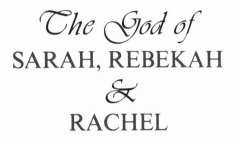

The God of
SARAH, REBEKAH
&
RACHEL

The God of
SARAH, REBEKAH
&
RACHEL

Barbara Keener Shenk

Foreword by A. Grace Wenger

Illustrated by Sibyl Graber Gerig

HERALD PRESS
Scottdale, Pennsylvania
Kitchener, Ontario
1985

Scripture quotations, except as otherwise noted, are condensed
from the *Holy Bible: New International Version.* Copyright © 1973
1978, 1984 by the International Bible Society. Used by permission
of Zondervan Bible Publishers.

THE GOD OF SARAH, REBEKAH, AND RACHEL
Copyright © 1985 by Herald Press, Scottdale, Pa. 15683
    Published simultaneously in Canada by Herald Press,
    Kitchener, Ont. N2G 4M5. All rights reserved.
Library of Congress Catalog Card Number: 85-5503
International Standard Book Number: 0-8361-3392-7
Printed in the United States of America

Design by Ann M. Graber

90 89 88 87 86 85 10 9 8 7 6 5 4 3 2 1

To Harriet with love and to other daughters
of Sarah, Rebekah, Rachel, and Leah

Contents

PART 1
Selections

PART 2
Complete Collection

Foreword

The women of the Bible speak in these sonnets.
Readers will hear the voices of those they know well: Eve in
the gossamer light of Eden, Ruth discovering that shared
sorrow becomes joy, Queen Esther rejoicing that she saved
her people.

Those, too, whose names are easily overlooked in the
histories, chronicles, and prophecies, step out to tell their
stories. Here is an opportunity to meet such interesting
people as Rebekah's grandmother Milcah, Joseph's wife
Asenath, Hannah's rival Peninnah, and Zeresh, the
ambitious wife of Haman.

The nameless ones, as well, become living women: the
unmarried daughters of Zelophehad, the mother of Icabod,
the wives of Ezekiel and of Nebuchadnezzar, the
concubines in King David's harem, and the women in the
besieged cities of Thebez and Abel Beth Maacah.

Even the most familiar figures appear in new light as
they speak for themselves. Noah's wife aches to finger a
garden, Jephthah's daughter hopes there will be a meadow
in the sky, and Queen Vashti's mask of pride hides shyness.
The reader meets Job's young daughters after their parents'
troubles have become history and glimpses the restlessness
that drives Gomer to be unfaithful to Hosea.

13

Today's women will recognize their own emotions of joy and bitterness, fulfillment and frustration, jealousy and devotion, gratitude and resentment, pride and self-pity, worry and fear, and uncertainty when loyalties conflict. The women who speak out of the past fear the situations met by women everywhere: the social stigma of being a criminal's wife, the realization that one's carelessness has crippled a child, the difficulty of being married to a visionary, the trouble that comes when parents show favoritism. A foster mother speaks, and so does the natural mother giving up her child to another woman. A mother watches for her son to return from war.

There are single women in a world dominated by men, a young girl forced into an alliance with an old man, and an abused woman returning to her abuser because she had nowhere else to go. There are happy women too, discovering the excitement of first love, enjoying quiet satisfaction as a second wife, or finding that a shared spiritual experience can bring new life to a marriage.

Yet, although they voice the emotions of universal womanhood, the women of the Bible have not been falsely modernized and Americanized. Their speeches have the ring of truth.

The sensitivity of the writer touches every page. Those who have known her as student, teacher, or friend remember her ability to respond, with sympathy and intelligence, to their feelings and her honesty in sharing her own emotions. Her strong sons and gracious daughters, in their caring for others, reflect the emotional climate of the home she and her husband have built. All of us who have lived, studied, worked, visited, or worshiped with her know her as a lover of God and a lover of people. These qualities color her interpretations of the sinners and saints of long ago.

Not only the women of the Bible speak here. Used as a mouthpiece, they communicate the warmth of a modern sinner-saint, Barbara.

A. GRACE WENGER
Leola, Pennsylvania

Acknowledgments

With unflagging gratitude and a wry smile, I acknowledge my loving and gifted family, without whose constant listening, criticizing and censoring this book would have been finished in half the time—and with less than half the quality!

My typist, Anna Ruth Martin, and her husband, Donald, were a constant source of encouragement, as were John Brenneman and his wife, Lois, who checked on progress almost daily and proofread the manuscript. Grace Wenger, former teacher and present friend, opened the mysteries of poetry to me and was the first person who suggested that my writings might deserve publication.

To those, and to other friends whose reactions gave me incentive to persevere, I offer deeply felt thanks.

BARBARA KEENER SHENK

PART 1

Selections

ONG OF EDEN

The Lord God said, "It is not good for the man to be alone. I will make a helper suitable for him." Then the Lord God made a woman from the rib he had taken out of the man, and he brought her to the man. The man said,
"This is now bone of my bones and flesh of my flesh; she shall be called 'woman,' for she was taken out of man."
A man will leave his father and mother and be united to his wife, and they will become one flesh. The man and his wife were both naked, and felt no shame.

Genesis 2:18-25

Adam! Adam! I wondered who God meant
While he with gentleness led on. And then
I saw the man. Warm ripples came and went
Around my heart as Adam whispered, "Friend,
My woman, wife, the one to whom I'll cleave
Like every son, forsaking us, will walk
Away with his own bride but we won't leave
Our garden or Creator." Eager talk
About the pets, the trees, the stream and mist
Made admiration bloom. How could he know
So much and be, like God, so kind? We kissed,
Explored and laughed as love made wonder grow.

We worked and played in gossamer of light
That warmed and shielded us by day and night.

WOMAN'S FIRST LAMENT

The garden plants responded to our care

And God. The pruning kept us busy, six

Days out of every week, while here and there

The young ones played with animals, with sticks

And stones. Their motions sang to me of grace

In bodies blithe and free. The girls' and boys'

Maturities gave ample time and space

To welcome each new birth. How could such joys

Grow old to me? How could I long to know

The hidden secrets God reserved? No need

Remained unfilled but some days I would go

And gaze upon the tree that held the seed

Of knowledge in its fruit. Alas! The snake

Suggested doubt—then sin—for wisdom's sake.

VE, MOTHER OF ALL

I took the fruit with first my eyes, then hand—

The taste was good. I gave my man a bite

And knew that instant why God's good command

Reserved his tree. We cringed and felt our light

Evaporate like mist before the sun.

We turned our backs, uneasy with the sense

Of nudity and shame of what we'd done.

The pain of evil knowledge burned intense

And now—in fur, I sweat and squirm and itch.

To clothe us, God destroyed some gentle pets.

My man must leave my side for labor which

Fatigues. Each baby, born so close, now gets

Divided love and Adam never knows

How deep my worry—and desiring—goes.

WIFE OF CAIN

The Lord said [to Cain], "What have you done? Listen! Your brother's blood cries out to me from the ground. Now you are under a curse and driven from the ground, which opened its mouth to receive your brother's blood from your hand. When you work the ground, it will no longer yield it's crops for you. You will be a wanderer on the earth."

Then the Lord put a mark on Cain so that no one who found him would kill him. So Cain went out from the Lord's presence and lived in the land of Nod, east of Eden.

Genesis 4:10-16

I'm banished with my man, away from God

Away from Eden and the fruitful earth

Which drank in Abel's blood and here in Nod

Refuses her abundance that the birth

Of man first saw. There's talk of sevenfold

And seventy times more revenge, so I—

Like Zillah, Adah, Lamech, Cain—have told

Our children how it is. Why try to lie?

Cain bears the mark but neighbors, whispering

Draw back their skirts from me. Small children call

Like hooting owls while we who bear, unseen,

Our stigma's trace, cannot escape his fall.

The one who killed retains his right to life

While passing, living death, unto his wife.

 ATER WIFE

My ears were ringing with the sound of all

The hammering they did while pitchblende stank,

But when the creatures came without our call

We all trooped in and God pulled up the plank.

For weeks we floated—homeless in our home—

Until one feeding time, some sprouted seeds

Just made my fingers ache to handle loam.

Then God, who spoke to Noah, saw our needs,

Remembered us, and sent his breathing wind.

He hung a rainbow in the misty sky

So that no matter how creation sinned

A flood would never make all nations die.

But with no Garden, eight souls seem so few

To fill the earth and conquer it anew.

HAGAR, THE MAID

My mistress always told me what to do

So when she said, "Here's Abram," how was I,

A purchased servant maid, expected to

Escape? There was no choice but to comply

Without a question raised of rights or love;

And if, as Sarah charged, I grew aloof

I call to witness God who reigns above

That she respected neither me nor truth.

At first she claimed my fruit was on her tree;

Then when her season came, she had no use

For me or Ishmael. In verity

She banished us without a good excuse.

Bad consequences can remain to vex

A selfish calculating use of sex.

Now Sarai, Abram's wife, had borne him no children. But she had an Egyptian maidservant named Hagar; so she said to Abram, "Go, sleep with my maidservant; perhaps I can build a family through her." Abram agreed to what Sarai said. He slept with Hagar, and she conceived.

But Sarah saw that the son whom Hagar the Egyptian had borne to Abraham was mocking, and she said to Abraham, "Get rid of that slave woman and her son, for that slave woman's son will never share in the inheritance with Isaac."

Genesis 16 and 21
Genesis 17:5, 15

26

LOT'S WIFE

I was embarrassed by my husband's greed

When Uncle Abram offered him a choice

Between hard work and riches, without need

Of grinding toil. But then I did rejoice

To have the social life for all our girls

Because I thought ahead of marriages.

At first, I felt some shock to see the curls,

The finery, the gleaming carriages;

But mothers must adjust and Lot was glad

For fertile pasturelands and for new friends

Who call him brother. You can see we had

A good life here, but now you say it ends.

You men are people we don't even know.

Who said you have the right to make us go?

27

LOT'S DAUGHTER

*Lot and his two daughters left
Zoar and settled in the mountains,
for he was afraid to stay in Zoar.
He and his two daughters lived in a
cave. One day the older daughter
said to the younger, "Our father is
old, and there is no man around
here to lie with us, as is the custom
all over the earth. Let's get our
father to drink wine and then lie
with him and preserve our family
line through our father." So both of
Lot's daughters became pregnant
by their father.*

Genesis 19:30-36

I wonder if my father felt remorse

For offering our virgin bodies to

His fellow Sodomites who came to force

Themselves, in lust, upon the strangers who

Had taken refuge underneath our roof;

Those visitors, in spite of sisters' men

Who mocked, gave all the rest of us the truth

About the home we'd never see again.

Does he remember them, so kind yet grim,

While Mother watered plants and fed the cat?

And now that we are both with child to him

What does my righteous parent think of that?

Although no one will ask the father's name

I look at Baby Moab's face with shame.

SARAH'S THANKSGIVING

Terah took his son Abram, his grandson Lot son of Haran, and his daughter-in-law Sarai from Ur of the Chaldeans to go to Canaan. But when they came to Haran, they settled there. Abram left (Haran), as the Lord had told him; and Lot went with him.

God also said to Abraham, "As for Sarai your wife, her name will be Sarah. I will bless her so that she will be the mother of nations; kings of peoples will come from her."

Look to Abraham, your father, and to Sarah, who gave you birth.

**Genesis 11, 12, and 17
Isaiah 51:2**

Our father, Terah, took us out of Ur

But settled down in Haran. Abram moved

Us on to fill the Promised Land. We were

Still childless and, in haste, I felt behooved

To mate my husband with my maid. That one ·

Mistake forced us to banish Ishmael

To clear the birthright for our promised son.

And Lord, who kept me safe in harem cell,

I thank you that you knew my feeble strength

And never spoke of sacrifice to me

When I held Isaac to my heart at length.

Because, Jehovah God, in honesty,

Although I traveled patiently through life,

It's hard to be a visionary's wife.

REBEKAH

What memories I have of leaving home

To comfort Isaac in his mother's tent,

Of nights we counted stars in heaven's dome

While pondering Jehovah's covenant.

I don't know when we first began to view

The twins with evil partiality;

But seeds, once planted, put out roots and grew

Until a tangle is surrounding me.

How can conspiracy be unconspired

Or half truth, loosely spoken, be made whole?

If pottery could ever be unfired

A liar might escape travail of soul.

I've listened for his step—but now I know

That Jacob will not come before I go.

LEAH'S LAMENT

Jacob was in love with Rachel and said, "I'll work for you seven years in return for your younger daughter Rachel."

When morning came, there was Leah! So Jacob said, "Why have you deceived me?" Laban replied, "We will give you the younger one also, in return for another seven years of work."

When the Lord saw that Leah was not loved, he opened her womb. Leah gave birth to a son. She named him Reuben, for she said, "Surely my husband will love me now."

Genesis 29:18-32

You, Rachel, you the ever favored one,

Why can't the watered palm tree be content

To furnish shade? Why pester for a son

When you already know that fate is bent

On serving you with joy and comradeship?

I only heard endearments one night through.

From Jacob's well of love, I got one sip

But every word he said was meant for you.

My helpless longing and my private shame

Of alternating hope and black despair

Are made more public every time I name

My sons—expecting now to be held dear.

I would give anything I have in life

To be my husband Jacob's only wife.

RACHEL TO LEAH

And Jacob did so. He finished
out the week with Leah, and then
Laban gave him his daughter
Rachel. Jacob lay with Rachel also,
and he loved Rachel more than
Leah. And he worked for Laban
another seven years.

Rachel began to give birth and
had great difficulty. And as she was
having great difficulty in childbirth,
the midwife said to her, "Don't be
afraid, for you have another son."
As she breathed her last—for she
was dying—she named her son Ben-
Oni. But his father named him
Benjamin.

Genesis 29:28-30; 35:16-18

While facing death, life passes for review:

I see those early days of childlike play

Replaced by rivalry and fears. It's true

I hid our father's gods, and in his way,

Well learned from him, deceived him by a ruse.

But can you, Leah, after years of pain

Imagine how I felt at his excuse

For giving you my wedding veil? In vain

I tried to make him yield the payment due,

But he just fed our jealous fire more wood.

Now Deborah's dead and I must turn to you,

My friend, and enemy, for my son's good.

If poor Ben-Oni lives (I hope he does)

Help him be stronger than his mother was.

ASENATH, WIFE OF JOSEPH

Although my childhood held bright hours of play,

The temple shadows often made me quake.

The idol caused my heart no fear by day,

But nightmares used to startle me awake.

Then as my girlish body showed some bloom

I wondered to what man I'd be assigned

And if my marriage would become my doom.

But Joseph holds my body, soul, and mind;

He tells our boys about the ways of sheep

With tender stories of his home, of dreams,

A special coat, and God who needs no sleep.

His love is inexhaustible, it seems.

Before he came, my chance of joy was slim—

My father's god can't make a man like him.

Pharaoh gave Joseph Asenath daughter of Potiphera, priest of On, to be his wife.

Before the years of famine came, two sons were born to Joseph by Asenath daughter of Potiphera, priest of On. Joseph named his firstborn Manasseh and said, "It is because God has made me forget all my trouble and all my father's household." The second son he named Ephraim and said, "It is because God has made me fruitful in the land of my suffering."

Genesis 41:45, 50-52

SONG OF THE MIDWIVES

We sing a song of children, ones and tens

Of scores and hundreds, plus uncounted more—

Nobody's lovers, everybody's friends

Because we helped with babies. Sorrow tore

Us both when infants were born dead. But worse

Than stillborns were the healthy ones who died.

We did our best. Sometimes we could reverse

The laws. If not, they had to be defied.

God's future leaders had been saved by us

And solitary parents here and there.

Then quietly, without a public fuss,

He started homes for us, with sons to bear.

Far greater than the wisdom of the wise

Is God, from whom deliverance will rise.

The king of Egypt said to the Hebrew midwives, whose names were Shiphrah and Puah, "When you help the Hebrew women in childbirth and observe them on the delivery stool, if it is a boy, kill him, but if it is a girl, let her live." The midwives, however, feared God and did not do what the king of Egypt had told them to do; they let the boys live. So God was kind to the midwives and the people increased and became even more numerous. And because the midwives feared God, he gave them families of their own.

Exodus 1:15-21

JOCHEBED

It seems as though the sun, so long kept out,

Now leaps with joy across the sill—like cats

Who wait for open doors. The children shout

In freedom at their play. While buzz of gnats

And Miriam's lilting song blend in my ears,

My happy fingers trace the royal mark

The princess placed upon our house. Old fears

Have melted since God used my little ark.

The princess was most gracious when I left

My son—and hers—at his new home today.

I kneel beside his empty bed, bereft,

But plan to use my extra time to pray.

At royal schools he'll learn things God can use

But when he's grown, I wonder how he'll choose.

PRINCESS OF EGYPT

Then Pharaoh's daughter went
down to the Nile to bathe. She saw
the basket among the reeds and sent
her slave girl to get it.

"This is one of the Hebrew
babies," she said.

Then his sister asked Pharaoh's
daughter, "Shall I go and get one of
the Hebrew women to nurse the
baby for you?"

"Yes, go," she answered. And the
girl went and got the baby's mother.
When the child grew older, she took
him to Pharaoh's daughter and he
became her son. She named him
Moses.

Exodus 2:5-10

I love the beneficial Mother Nile

For worship, bathing, and fertility.

Of course I fear her son, the Crocodile,

Whose bloody teeth are schooled in cruelty

Used often now, since Father made his law

About the Hebrew boys. My drawn-out one

Is special. There's no way to save them all

But his wet nurse and I preserved my son.

Without his foster mother he would die

Or without me. He must learn everything

From magic arts, from earth and from the sky

Because he'll someday reign as Egypt's king.

O God of ancient lore and hidden ways,

Help Moses be your servant all his days.

MIRIAM'S THANKSGIVING

Jochebed bore Aaron, Moses and their sister Miriam.

Miriam the prophetess, Aaron's sister, took a tambourine in her hand, and Miriam sang to them.

Miriam and Aaron began to talk against Moses. When the cloud lifted from above the Tent, there stood Miriam—leprous, like snow. So Moses cried out to the Lord, "O God, please heal her!"

I brought you up out of Egypt. I sent Moses to lead you, also Aaron and Miriam.

Numbers 26:29; Exodus 15:20-21; Numbers 12:1-13; Micah 6:4

I often left my fun to play with him

And quiet every whimper from his bed

Lest baby-hunters by design or whim

Should find out where he lay. He would be dead

According to the Pharaoh's plan—not God's

Who favored little brother from his birth;

So while our men folks bore the bricks and rods,

I helped my mother teach God's man, his worth.

When as his helper, I—and Aaron too—

Because of lesser honors, felt abused

And told our younger brother what to do,

We learned by Moses' love why he was used.

I'm glad, in spite of all the times I fell

That God made me a gift to Israel.

RAHAB, SALMON'S WIFE

Two spies entered the house of a prostitute named Rahab and stayed there. She went up on the roof and said to them, "Please swear to me by the Lord that you will show kindness to my family." The men said to her, "This oath will not be binding on us unless you have tied this scarlet cord in the window and unless you have brought your family into your house."

* * *

The young men who had done the spying went in and brought out Rahab and all who belonged to her.

Joshua 2:1-18; 6:23

They came at night, as customers would do

But in a moment I could see that this

Was not a business call. They were the two

Most courteous of men. I could not miss

The chance to save my kindred young and old,

And so I made them promise for the Lord

That they would spare my gathered-in household

And I would keep our secret of the cord.

I had a tent and learned to pitch it well

Until—Jehovah's mercies never cease—

I got to be a wife in Israel

And, by my husband's lineage—Aaron's niece.

I'm glad God looks at what a person does

And judges who I am—not who I was.

CSAH, DAUGHTER AND WIFE

Our camp is like a forest of young trees

Where Joshua and Father soar alone

Like two strong cedars standing firm to please

The Lord. For Father, trials served to hone

A sharper, cutting edge of faith to use

In conquest of the Promised Land. What's more,

At eighty-five, he never did excuse

Himself from working hard or waging war.

According to his offer of my hand

For any man who led the battle strife,

Dear Othniel and I received good land

With springs, when I became the hero's wife.

But I remember best that Father's eyes

Saw me as precious—fit to be a prize.

And Caleb said, "I will give my daughter Acsah in marriage to the man who attacks and captures Kiriath Sepher." Othniel son of Kenaz, Caleb's younger brother, took it; so Caleb gave his daughter Acsah to him in marriage. One day when she came to Othniel, she urged him to ask her father for a field. When she got off her donkey, Caleb asked her, "What can I do for you?"

She replied, "Do me a special favor. Since you have given me land in the Negev, give me also springs of water."

Judges 1:12-15

45

DAUGHTERS OF ZELOPHEHAD

Now Zelophehad son of Hepher, the son of Gilead, the son of Makir, the son of Manasseh, had no sons but only daughters, whose names were Mahlah, Noah, Hoglah, Milcah and Tirzah. They went to Eleazar the priest, Joshua son of Nun, and the leaders and said, "The Lord commanded Moses to give us an inheritance among our brothers." So Joshua gave them an inheritance along with the brothers of their father, according to the Lord's cammand.

Joshua 17:3-6

Because our Father's gone, the years look bleak

With five of us to marry, hopefully,

And no male relatives that care to speak

For us, or save our lives from drudgery.

We've gathered manna with the rest and pitched

Our tent as well as any man, but now

We need some help, or we will all be nitched

In corners where the folks make room somehow.

We feel our worth and know we are as good

As those who keep a clean and happy house,

But where's a modest way by which we could

Attract, for each of us, a worthy spouse?

We praise Jehovah who has made it known

That single girls need land to call their own.

MOTHER OF SISERA

How dare the moonlight sweep beneath our gate
Before my Sisera comes flashing in
From slaughtering those Hebrew sheep. It's late
And I had thought that he would quickly win
With chariots of iron and horses trained
To scatter men on foot, like quail. We heard
With scorn of Barak. Yet, my son's detained
By someone. Very soon he'll send us word.
The spoil should be divided now. Two slaves
For him, one maiden for another. Cloth
Embroidered on both sides, he always saves
For me—Oh, fear, stop fanning like a moth.

Is there no word of hope or sure relief
For window-watching women, fearing grief?

"Through the window peered Sisera's mother; behind the lattice she cried out, 'Why is his chariot so long in coming? Why is the clatter of his chariots delayed?'

"The wisest of her ladies answer her; indeed, she keeps saying to herself, 'Are they not finding and dividing the spoils; a girl or two for each man, colorful garments as plunder for Sisera, colorful garments embroidered, for my neck—all this as plunder?' "

Judges 5:28-30

DEBORAH

Accumulated wisdom through the years
Unfolding like palm leaves from my own tree
Has helped me make decisions, handle fears,
And triumph in the work God gave. When we
Were frightened off the main highways and hid
Like rabbits in a hole, Barak said, "Go
With me or I won't go at all!" I did,
Although, as wife and mother, I don't know
The general's part or how to wield a sword;
But we, together, with ten thousand men
Saw chariots run, like mice, before the Lord.
Then I went home to Lappidoth again.

When God selects the one he wants to ask
He gives ability to do the task.

Deborah, a prophetess, the wife of Lappidoth, was leading Israel. She held court under the Palm of Deborah. She sent for Barak and said to him, "The Lord, the God of Israel, commands you: 'Go, take with you ten thousand men. I will lure Sisera and give him into your hands.'"

* * *

Barak said to her, "If you go with me, I will go; but if you don't go with me, I won't go."

"Very well," Deborah said, "I will go with you."

Judges 4:4-9

EPHTHAH'S DAUGHTER

When Jephthah returned, who should come out to meet him but his daughter, dancing. When he saw her, he tore his clothes and cried, "Oh! My daughter! You have made me miserable and wretched, because I have made a vow to the Lord that I cannot break."

"My father," she replied, "Do to me just as you promised. But give me two months to roam the hills and weep with my friends." After the two months, she returned to her father and he did to her as he had vowed.

Judges 11:34-39

My father promised, so there is no chance

For me, unless I'd make him break his vow

To God. I had no way to know my dance

Of joy could spring a trap of doom. But now

I must return—while feeling like a brook

Whose waters will not ever join the sea,

Or like a fuzzy eaglet in a nook

Whose wings will never grow to set it free.

I wonder who will finger those designs

That Father carved into my ivory bed

And if they'll find that no one really minds

My little puppy's mischief when I'm dead.

I hope God has a meadow in the sky

For us who leave the earth too young to die.

MOTHER OF SAMSON

A certain man named Manoah had a wife who was sterile. The angel of the Lord appeared to her and said, "You are going to conceive and have a son. Now see to it that you drink no wine. No razor may be used on his head. He will begin the deliverance of Israel." Samson led Israel for twenty years in the days of the Philistines.

Then [after his experience with Delilah] the Philistines seized him, gouged out his eyes and set him to grinding in the prison.

Judges 13:2-5; 16:21

Our hearts ascended with the angel's flame

Till he evaporated from our sight

And left us with our wonder but no name

For him or for our future child who might

Deliver Israel for the Lord. Our joy

Increased with gratitude that God had shown

His own prophetic will about our boy

And gave him power none of us had known.

Then grapes, forbidden, turned to wine of wrath

Because our son persistently would seek

For honey in a hornet's nest—a path

To prison where he's shorn, and blind, and weak.

When we remember Samson, young and strong,

Our minds keep asking, "Where did we go wrong?"

ELILAH'S REGRET

Some time later, he fell in love with a woman whose name was Delilah. The rulers of the Philistines went and said, "See if you can lure him into showing how we may tie and subdue him. Each one of us will give you eleven hundred shekels of silver."

Delilah said, "Tell me the secret of your great strength and how you can be subdued."

Samson answered her, "If anyone ties me with seven fresh thongs that have not been dried, I'll become as weak as any other man." But he snapped the thongs as easily as a piece of string snaps when it comes close to a flame. So the

The Hebrew man, with country charm and ways

Of pleasing that I never knew, was still

My enemy. The busy nights and days

Were pieces of a master plan to kill

The happy fly while keeping from his sight

My secret spider web. Of course by law

Poor Samson's downfall was the only right

And patriotic duty that I saw.

I'm wealthy now, renowned, and booked ahead

By politicians, priests, and famous men

Yet I would rather have him free instead.

I would not be so treacherous again.

But time has healed my wound—or so I thought

Until that day I cracked the vase he brought.

secret of his strength was not discovered.

"If anyone ties me securely with new ropes that have never been used, I'll become as weak as any other man." But he snapped the ropes off his arms as if they were threads.

"If you weave the seven braids of my head into the fabric on the loom and tighten it with the pin, I'll become as weak as any other man." He awoke from his sleep and pulled up the pin and the loom, with the fabric.

Then she said to him, "How can you say, 'I love you,' when you won't confide in me? This is the third time you have made a fool of me and haven't told me the secret of your great strength."

With such nagging she prodded him day after day until he was tired to death. So he told everything. "No razor has ever been used on my head," he said, "because I have been a Nazirite set apart to God since birth. If my head were shaved, my strength would leave me, and I would become as weak as any other man."

"Come back once more; he has told me everything." So the rulers of the Philistines returned with the silver in their hands. Having put him to sleep on her lap, she called a man to shave off the seven braids of his hair, and so began to subdue him. But the hair on his head began to grow again.

Samson prayed to the Lord. Then he pushed with all his might, and down came the temple. And his father's whole family buried him. He had led Israel twenty years.

Judges 16:4-31

HE LEVITE'S CONCUBINE

Some of the wicked men of the city surrounded the house. "Bring out the man who came to your house so we can have sex with him."

"No, my friends, don't be so vile. Look, here is my virgin daughter, and his concubine, use them."

But the men would not listen to him. So the man took his concubine and sent her outside to them, and they raped her and abused her throughout the night. In the morning there lay his concubine with her hands on the threshold.

Judges 19:1-27

I wish I never would have come along
With him in spite of all the kindliness
He showed in conversation. Warnings—strong
And menacing at night—would seem much less
Important when the sun was high and he
Could be persuaded to postpone again
Our final leaving—which was hard for me,
But nothing like the hardship of these men.
How could he offer me, to serve their lust
While knowing I have been afraid of him?
A woman has to do the things she must,
But times like this can overflow the brim.

I'm crawling back to find his step. I know
That he's no help, but where else could I go?

ORPAH

Naomi and her daughters-in-law
prepared to return.

Then Naomi said to her two
daughters-in-law, "Go back, each of
you. May the Lord grant that each
of you will find rest in the home of
another husband."

"We will go back with you to
your people."

"Why would you come with me?
Even if I had a husband tonight and
then gave birth to sons would you
remain unmarried for them? No,
my daughters." Then Orpah kissed
her mother-in-law good-bye.

Ruth 1:6-14

Our sleepy village woke if visitors

Began to climb our winding, rocky way

So now, although most memories are blurs

I still can see the details of the day

Naomi came. Of course, when I met her

I never dreamed that I would be the wife

Of one my people labeled, "foreigner."

Nor that his death would devastate my life.

Another son from her is, as she said,

Not really now a possibility;

In spite of love, I will return instead

And hope that there is future rest for me.

The bread of yesterday will not suffice

If here today, I have no loaf to slice.

UTH TO NAOMI *AFTER OBED*

I still remember you on that first day

With sweat streaks on your face and wilted from

The dusty road. I wanted you to stay

And use our village as your shelter. Some

Of us were watching how you calmly talked

Among yourselves with gentleness and I

Was most impressed by how your husband walked

Beside you and my heart could feel the tie.

Then as I joined the circle of your love,

Your inner flame warmed me and helped me see

That loyalty and truth form bonds above

My childhood thoughts and last eternally.

I came to share your bitter dregs with you

And found the cup was filled with joy for two.

AOMI *AFTER OBED*

Naomi was left without her two sons and her husband.

"Look," said Naomi, "your sister-in-law is going back to her people and her gods. Go back with her." Ruth was determined. So the two women went on until they came to Bethlehem [where] the women exclaimed, "Can this be Naomi?" She told them, "Call me Mara, because the Almighty has made my life very bitter."

* * *

The women said, "Your daughter-in-law, who loves you and who is better to you than seven sons, has given him [Obed] birth."

Ruth 1:3-20; 4:14-15

In happiness and health I felt my life

Was moving like a quiet stream where sheep

Could safely wade. To be a chosen wife,

I found, was like a pond, so clear and deep

That quietness could reign. When God gave sons

He taught us that the ripples catch the light

And streams with hidden music are the ones

That tumble over rocks. Then came the night.

I felt deserted on a beach of sand,

Until in Moab each son found a bride

And briefly shared his home. By death, the hand

Of God once more swept joy and hope aside.

Through Ruth, I see that life is like a shore

And joy can sweep where grief tides ran before.

PENINNAH, HANNAH'S RIVAL

Although my man is good and knows the law

So he does not diminish food or clothes

Or duty of the marriage bond, I saw

Again how he, by worthy portion, shows

In public that she is much more preferred.

But I can nurse my babies in her sight

And by well-chosen toss of head or word

Make sure she shares my shadow day and night.

I think of Zilpah, Bilhah—concubines

Or wives, by name, but not by what we mean.

We know a barrenness;—there are two kinds!

The one, we feel, when we give birth or wean.

In spite of pretense, sham, and outer life

There's pain in every loved-by-duty wife.

HANNAH

Peninnah had children, but Hannah had none. Elkanah her husband would say, "Don't I mean more to you than ten sons?"

In bitterness of soul Hannah wept much and prayed to the Lord, "O Lord Almighty, if you will only look upon your servant's misery and remember me, and not forget your servant but give her a son, then I will give him to the Lord for all the days of his life."

Hannah gave birth. And the Lord was gracious to Hannah. The boy Samuel grew up in the presence of the Lord.

1 Samuel 1:2, 8-11, 20; 2:21

To want a child like deserts long for rain
And have a restlessness like ocean's tide
Would be enough, if private. But the pain
Of mean Peninnah's gloating, throbs beside
The knowledge that in cruelty she spoke
So everyone would know. A man can sow
Good seed in willing earth and wait in hope,
But only God has power to make it grow.
That's why I went to him with breaking heart
For fruit and for the clearing of my name.
Praise God, he heard. Now I must do my part
So that my son will never bring us shame.

The way I spend these years that fly so fast
Will make me full or empty when they're past.

66

ITCH OF ENDOR

When Saul saw the Philistine army, he was afraid. He inquired of the Lord, but the Lord did not answer. Saul then said to his attendants, "Find me a woman who is a medium."

"There is one in Endor," [*they* answered].

The woman said to him, "Why have you set a trap for my life to bring about my death?"

Saul swore to her by the Lord, "You will not be punished." When the woman saw Samuel, she cried out at the top of her voice and said to Saul, "Why have you deceived me? You are Saul!"

1 Samuel 28:5-14

These hands have mastered chores they never knew

Before, and vegetables are growing in

My patch, because when Saul was asking who

The witches were to kill them for their sin

I was a former witch that very day

With my own goat to milk and hens to feed,

As I began to live a better way

Of freedom from the devil and from need.

But now, with fear, I face the sudden fact

That flashed across my mind when Samuel spoke:

My power with the spirits is intact

And I am locked into a double yoke.

It's too late now, for me. I can't negate

The deal with Lucifer that sealed my fate.

URSE FOR MEPHIBOSHETH

(Jonathan son of Saul had a son who was lame in both feet. He was five years old when the news about Saul and Jonathan came from Jezreel. His nurse picked him up and fled, but as she hurried to leave, he fell and became crippled. His name was Mephibosheth.)

2 Samuel 4:4

To be a nursemaid for the king is hard

Because his children are in danger day

And night. When they are playing in their yard

I'm like a hen with chicks and always pray

That neither dangers from the earth nor sky

Will change their vibrant health or introduce

A threat to life or limb. I hear each cry

With dread lest enemies are on the loose.

And then it happened as I feared it would:

One night—when all the children were in bed.

I snatched Mephibosheth and what I could

Of things he'd need—then dropped him as I fled.

Through years of sorrow, I've bewailed his fate:

Because of my misstep, he can't walk straight.

ATHSHEBA WHISPERS

One evening David got up from his bed and walked around on the roof of the palace. From the roof he saw a woman bathing.

[It was] "Bathsheba, the daughter of Eliam and the wife of Uriah."

Then David sent messengers to get her. She came to him, and he slept with her. The woman conceived and sent word.

[After Uriah refused to go home to be with Bathsheba] David wrote a letter to Joab: "Put Uriah in the front line where the fighting is fiercest. Then withdraw from him so he will die.

2 Samuel 11:2-15

The tree Uriah planted in our yard

I see in moonlight from my present house.

Entranced by breezes in his tree, it's hard

For me to sort my thoughts of him—the spouse

Who loved his king and battle comrades more

Sometimes than me. Or so at least it seemed,

Until the death of David's son made sure

Some things of which I'd only vaguely dreamed.

When God sent Nathan, who exposed our wrong,

He made us deal in truth instead of lies.

So now my faith for Solomon is strong;

O God, please use my life to make him wise.

I can't feel guiltless for our trysting night;

My bathing never should have been in sight.

73

ELEAGUERED BY WAR

We cannot stand to see armed men outside
Our wall and know that they have come for war,
Expecting to involve those who abide
In peace and harmlessness. And what is more,
Though women are the ones who wait in vain
For sons and husbands from the battlefield,
It's worse when selfishness brings seige and pain
Right to our household doors. We will not yield
Or sacrifice those loved since their first move
Within the womb before we'd swaddled, fed,
And cherished them. It therefore does behoove
A man attacking homes to watch his head.

The battles usually are fought by men
But it's not wise to raid a grizzly's den.

TEN ROYAL CONCUBINES

The king [departed] but he left ten concubines. Absalom said to Ahithophel, "Give us your advice. What should we do?" Ahithophel answered, "Lie with your father's concubines."

They pitched a tent for Absalom on the roof, and he lay with his father's concubines.

When David returned he took the ten concubines he had left to take care of the palace and put them under guard. He provided for them, but did not lie with them. They were kept in confinement living as widows.

2 Samuel 15:16; 16:20-22; 20:3

Conspiracy and flight left us in charge
Of David's palace when he fled unshod
With all the rest, while anyone could barge
In where we huddled—be he prince or clod.
They pulled us out like rabbits from a hole
And Absalom wrought shame beneath a tent
In public view. To purchase his new role
As self-made king, we were the coins he spent.

While years of our confinement stretch ahead
As though we all were guilty of some crime,
Our guards, by order, see that we are fed
Until death will release us all, in time.
But we, as chattel women, spend our days
In ward, while flocks and herds go out to graze.

THE WILLING WENCH

Ahithophel avenged Bathsheba's shame
When Absalom so openly disgraced
His father's concubines and royal name
While barefoot David fled in weeping haste.
Now spies and counterspies lurk out of sight;
Two men who feign allegiance stay at court
And learn how Absalom intends to fight—
But they need help to carry their report.
No wife or daughter from this priestly house
Can safely leave the city undisguised.
But I, a bonded wench, drab as a mouse,
Will use the liberty of one despised.

Nobility, when measured by the deed,
Is not confined to those of noble seed.

Then said Hushai unto Zadok and to Abiathar the priests, Thus and thus did Ahithophel counsel Absalom and the elders of Israel; and tell David, saying, Lodge not this night in the plains of the wilderness, but speedily pass over; lest the king be swallowed up, and all the people that are with him. Now Jonathan and Ahimaaz stayed by Enrogel; for they might not be seen to come into the city: and a wench went and told them.

2 Samuel 17:15-17 (KJV)

WIFE OF JEROBOAM

Ahijah son of Jeroboam became ill, and Jeroboam said to his wife, "Go to Shiloh. Ahijah the prophet will tell you what will happen to the boy."

Ahijah said, "Come in, wife of Jeroboam. I have been sent to you with bad news. Go, tell Jeroboam, 'You have done more evil than all who lived before you. You have made for yourself other gods, idols made of metal; you have provoked me to anger.'

"As for you, go back home. When you set foot in your city, the boy will die."

1 Kings 14:1-20

He could contrive imaginary gods
When politics and kingdoms were at stake,
But with our son so sick, my husband plods
In mental valleys where the buzzards make
Their patient, measured wheelings in the sky.
At Jeroboam's word, I have to go
To find out if our son will live or die—
And who else but the man of God will know?

I shrank back from the prophet's scalding word
And melted like a candle on his floor.
I cannot change the message that I heard;
Our boy will die when I approach my door.
My journey home winds up his life like thread
And just before I reach him, he'll be dead.

79

ZUBAH, WIFE OF ASA

Asa did what was right in the eyes of the Lord, as his father David had done. He expelled the male shrine prostitutes from the land and got rid of all the idols his fathers had made. He even deposed his grandmother Maacah from her position as queen mother, because she had made a repulsive Asherah pole. Asa's heart was fully committed to the Lord all his life.

Jehoshaphat son of Asa became king of Judah in the fourth year of Ahab king of Israel. His mother's name was Azubah.

1 Kings 15:11-14; 22:41-42

Possessively, I wake and watch him sleep

Almost in disbelief. I lift my man

In supplication too, that God will keep

Him safe from every diabolic plan

With which the devil may retaliate

For Asa's turning Judah back to God

And throwing idols down. I fear the hate

From displaced Sodomites who felt his rod

Of righteous indignation. Like a knife

My terror wants to clip his eagle wings

Till I remember I am just his wife;

But he is subject to the king of kings.

I wonder if all men who fill a throne

Have proud and fearful wives who feel alone.

HOSTESS OF SHUNEM

The passing prophet now stops here for bread

Since I, at first, constrained him when I saw

With deep respect his age and balding head,

And thought to make a room upon our wall

Where he could feel that he had found a nest,

In readiness, each time that he came back.

And when he wondered what reward was best

For me, I truthfully could feel no lack.

But that was changed when we received the son

He promised. Evening time demands no light

Until the candle's lit, but once begun

And then snuffed out, its absence brings on night.

Since we saw life and death, we now know more

About the Lord of life, who can restore.

QUEEN ATHALIAH

When Athaliah the mother of Ahaziah saw that her son was dead, she proceeded to destroy the whole royal family. But Jehosheba took Joash. He remained hidden with his nurse at the temple of the Lord for six years while Athaliah ruled the land. In the seventh year Jehoiada sent for the commanders. He made a covenant with them and showed them the king's son. Jehoiada put the crown on him. They shouted, "Long live the king!" Athaliah tore her robes and called out, "Treason! Treason!"

2 King 11:1-14

Now that my son the former king is dead

I'll just exterminate the royal seed

And put the crown of Judah on my head

Before I hint of any change. I'll need

A few well-seasoned, bloody men to clear

The world of heirs and rid me in one day

Of any competition I might fear.

We'll move so swiftly none will get away.

How after years of reigning as a queen

Could I hear shoutings of "God save the king"?

What does that childlike apparition mean,

And who has engineered this dreadful thing?

It's treason! Treason! Loyalty's at stake.

Have mercy on me, please, for Baal's sake.

HULDAH, THE PROPHETESS

While they were bringing out the money Hilkiah the priest found the Book of the Law of the Lord that had been given through Moses.

When the king heard the words he tore his robes. He gave these orders to Hilkiah, "Go and inquire of the Lord."

Hilkiah and those the king had sent with him went to speak to the prophetess Huldah, who was the wife of Shallum. She said to them, "Tell the man who sent you to me, 'This is what the Lord says: I am going to bring disaster on this place.'"

2 Chronicles 34:14-24

I'm glad my father shared with me the things

That other folks forgot or never knew

About the prophets, priests, successive kings—

Intrigue and evil, idols, and a few

Less public women who fulfilled their roles

Of ordinary life, but also heard

The secrets God reveals to waiting souls

Whose hearts are open to Jehovah's word.

Today Josiah's workmen found the law.

In urgency, bowed down by what they learned,

They trembled to my door for me to call

Upon the Lord of heaven they had spurned.

In time of need God told me what to say

Because I speak to him from day to day.

BUILDERS OF JERUSALEM

Then I said to them, "You see the trouble we are in: Jerusalem lies in ruins, and its gates have been burned with fire. Come, let us rebuild." They replied, "Let us start rebuilding." So they began this good work. But when Sanballat the Horonite, Tobiah the Ammonite official and Geshem the Arab heard about it, they mocked and ridiculed us.

* * *

Shallum son of Hallohesh, ruler of a half-district of Jerusalem, repaired the next section with the help of his daughters.

Nehemiah 2:17-20 and 3:12

Our heavy days are lightened by the zest

That conflict lends while we rebuild the wall;

And heathen neighbors do their crafty best

To hinder us with threats of force, and call

Insulting slurs of what a fox could do

By running up our masonry. We work

Without a break, and Nehemiah, who

Is ruler, watches enemies that lurk.

Each man has his assignment, with his sons,

And builds while keeping weapons by his hand.

But we, who have no brothers, are the ones

Who work with Father at the Lord's command.

The other workers might not take as long

But when we're done our wall is just as strong.

QUEEN VASHTI

He [Ahasuerus] gave a banquet for all his nobles and officials. He displayed the vast wealth of his kingdom and the splendor and glory of his majesty. When these days were over, the king gave [another] banquet.

Queen Vashti also gave a banquet for the women. On the seventh day, when King Xerxes [Ahasuerus] was in high spirits from wine, he commanded the seven eunuchs to bring Vashti to display her beauty to the people. But Queen Vashti refused to come.

Esther 1:1-12

I was his queen and I enjoyed the things

Ahasuerus whispered in my ear.

But acclamation is the way of kings

Who flaunt their treasures and who like to hear

That no one's wealth surpasses what they hold.

Yet my self-consciousness would chill me when

I feared the servants were too close, like cold

Spring wind makes fruit tree buds retreat again.

The day that we were each surrounded by

Our friends was not a time when even crowns

Could tempt a little rabbit—scared and shy—

To venture forth in front of baying hounds.

A woman does herself and others harm

By public exhibition of her charm.

ZERESH, WIFE OF HAMAN

Haman boasted about his vast wealth, his many sons, and ways the king had honored him.

* * *

Zeresh said to him, "Have a gallows built and ask the king to have Mordecai hanged on it."

* * *

Zeresh said, "Since Mordecai is of Jewish origin, you will surely come to ruin!"

* * *

They hanged Haman on the gallows he had prepared for Mordecai. "If it pleases the king," Esther [said], "Let Haman's ten sons be hanged on gallows."

Esther 5:10-14; 6:12, 13; 7:10; 9:13

I was as eager as a hound that trails
Small game to sniff out Haman's news of court
And his successes. Asking for details
Of queenly dress and menus, I'd resort
To any measure that gave me a part
In his exclusive closeness to the king,
Although I knew my husband's bitter heart
Was festering into a deadly thing.

With Haman gone, and ten sons murdered in
One day, I cower in an empty house
That's haunted by his gallows and the sin
Of my suggesting them to please my spouse.

A noble wife should take a moral stand
Before her husband's goals get out of hand.

ESTHER SPEAKS

They say I'm graceful as the willow trees,

But I feel much more like a sturdy oak

That men can burn or split or shape to please

When they have need. Since parents died, I spoke

To cousin Mordecai when I felt

My helplessness. I'm glad it's over now.

Jehovah made Ahasuerus melt

When I was sent to make my virgin bow

To circumstances and to him. Again

When Haman showed his hand, the king took mine

And made a proclamation to all men

Confirming rights of Jews, and fixed his sign.

By now, God's purposes are clearly seen

In having me become a pagan's queen.

JOB'S WIFE

I was Job's queen of generosity:

The more we gave, the more we seemed to get

Until our wealth surpassed reality

Yet still increased. I never will forget

The picture that the children made as they

Enjoyed their life together, taking turns

For each to entertain the others. Day

By day, Job was the one who felt concerns.

Our life exploded, while I blinked my eye.

I was the only thing God left to Job

And I, repulsed, told him to curse and die;

I played the fool and spurned the mourner's robe.

My soul stands shivering—stripped and alone—

To find that things meant more than I had known.

In the land of Uz there lived a man whose name was Job. He feared God and shunned evil.

His sons used to take turns holding feasts and they would invite their three sisters.

Job would sacrifice a burnt offering for each of them, "Perhaps my children have sinned and cursed God in their hearts."

Job said: "The Lord gave and the Lord has taken." In all this, Job did not sin.

His wife said to him, "Are you still holding on to your integrity? Curse God and die!"

Job 1:1—2:10

MMANUEL'S MOTHER

I felt that God confirmed my early choice

To be a virgin prophetess. Yet now

And then, as I would watch new brides rejoice,

I had to pray for strength to keep my vow

So that the Lord could always find my life

Available, without the daily chores

Or worries that are juggled by a wife

Who has no time to enter other doors.

O, how things changed the day Isaiah came

And called me highly favored as the one

God chose to be a sign. He shared a name

Which witnesses agreed was for our son.

So now when neighbors rail and gossips fuss

I whisper to my child, "God is with us."

When Ahaz was king the hearts of Ahaz and his people were shaken, as the trees of the forest are shaken by the wind. Then the Lord said to Isaiah, "Go out, you and your son Shear-Jashub, to meet Ahaz at the end of the aqueduct of the Upper Pool, on the road to the Washerman's Field. Say to him, 'Be careful, keep calm and don't be afraid. Do not lose heart because of these two smoldering stubs of firewood. This is what the Sovereign Lord says:

" 'It will not take place, it will not happen.' "

Again the Lord spoke to Ahaz, "Ask the Lord your God for a sign, whether in the deepest depths or in the highest heights."

But Ahaz said, "I will not ask; I will not put the Lord to the test."

Then Isaiah said, "Hear now, you house of David! Is it not enough to try the patience of men? Will you try the patience of God also? Therefore the Lord himself will give you a sign: The virgin will be with child and will give birth to a son, and will call him Immanuel. He will eat curds and honey when he knows enough to reject the wrong and choose the right. But before the boy knows enough to reject the wrong and choose the right, the land of the two kings you dread will be laid waste."

The Lord said to me, "Take a large scroll and write on it with an ordinary pen: Maher-Shalal-Hash-Baz. And I will call in Uriah the priest and Zechariah son of Jeberekiah as reliable witnesses for me." Then I went to the prophetess, and she conceived and gave birth to a son. And the Lord said, "Name him Maher-Shalal-Hash-Baz. Before the boy knows how to say 'My father' or 'My mother,' the

wealth of Damascus and the plunder of Samaria will be carried off." The Lord spoke to me again: "Because this people has rejected the gently flowing waters of Shiloah the Lord is about to bring against them the mighty flood waters of the River—

O Immanuel!"

Here am I, and the children the Lord has given me. We are signs and symbols in Israel from the Lord, who dwells on Mount Zion.

Isaiah 7:1-16; 8:1-8, and 18

THE CONSTANT LOVER

I've lost all track of time. How long have I

Been living in a room of draperies?

How long before I skip beneath a sky

Of fleecy sheeplike clouds, while grapes and trees

Perfume the air, and my betrothed claims me?

The king, my charge while he drew breath, is dead,

So after days of mourning I'll be free

For lilies, apples, and my nuptial bed.

The guards for Solomon made me return

As though I were inherited along

With David's throne. But inwardly, I yearn

To find my shepherd and renew our song.

Because the king could not destroy my love

I'm flying home—once more, a country dove.

David could not keep warm. So his servants said "Look for a young virgin to lie beside him so that our lord the king may keep warm."

Tell me, you whom I love, where you graze your flock and where you rest your sheep at midday. My lover is mine and I am his; he browses among the lilies. Until the day breaks and the shadows flee. Many waters cannot quench love; rivers cannot wash it away. If one were to give all the wealth of his house for love, it would be utterly scorned.

1 Kings 1:1-4
Song of Songs 1:7; 2:16; 8:7

GOMER, WIFE OF HOSEA

Hosea loves me faithfully and tends

The babies, sometimes, when he's able to,

So people wonder why I need my friends

When I already have a husband who

Keeps candles lighted while I'm gone; but still

There is a restlessness that prickles me

And hollows little cavities to fill

While scary dreams obscure reality.

He pleads with me for our three children's sake,

But doesn't hear me say that I'm a child.

To be so changeable is hard to take

And thoughts of bars and cages leave me wild.

I'm back, again—paid for in cash and grain.

The clouds are here. How long until the rain?

THE CLOUD OF WITNESSES

Our sorrow weeps in all the willow trees
And is distilled in every drizzling rain
While laughter's echoes float upon the breeze
That cools a summer day and eases pain.
When people press a conch against an ear
To catch the pounding rhythm of the sea,
It is our throbbing heart that they can hear,
And to some mysteries, we hold the key.
Our feelings which are soft as kitten fur
Are also sharp as any piercing thorn;
So thoughts of honey mingle with the myrrh
Each time we sense a child is newly born.

But questionings of life are in the past
Now that we know as we are known—at last.

PART 2

Complete Collection

SONG OF EDEN

Adam! Adam! I wondered who God meant
While he with gentleness led on. And then
I saw the man. Warm ripples came and went
Around my heart as Adam whispered, "Friend,
My woman, wife, the one to whom I'll cleave
Like every son, forsaking us, will walk
Away with his own bride but we won't leave
Our garden or Creator." Eager talk
About the pets, the trees, the stream and mist
Made admiration bloom. How could he know
So much and be, like God, so kind? We kissed,
Explored and laughed as love made wonder grow.

We worked and played in gossamer of light
That warmed and shielded us by day and night.

Genesis 1 and 2

WOMAN'S FIRST LAMENT

The garden plants responded to our care
And God. The pruning kept us busy, six
Days out of every week, while here and there
The young ones played with animals, with sticks
And stones. Their motions sang to me of grace
In bodies blithe and free. The girls' and boys'
Maturities gave ample time and space
To welcome each new birth. How could such joys
Grow old to me? How could I long to know
The hidden secrets God reserved? No need
Remained unfilled but some days I would go
And gaze upon the tree that held the seed
Of knowledge in its fruit. Alas! The snake
Suggested doubt—then sin—for wisdom's sake.

Genesis 3:1-6

EVE, MOTHER OF ALL

I took the fruit with first my eyes, then hand—
The taste was good. I gave my man a bite
And knew that instant why God's good command
Reserved his tree. We cringed and felt our light
Evaporate like mist before the sun.
We turned our backs, uneasy with the sense
Of nudity and shame of what we'd done.
The pain of evil knowledge burned intense
And now—in fur, I sweat and squirm and itch.
To clothe us, God destroyed some gentle pets.
My man must leave my side for labor which
Fatigues. Each baby, born so close, now gets
Divided love and Adam never knows
How deep my worry—and desiring—goes.

Genesis 3

WIFE OF CAIN

I'm banished with my man, away from God
Away from Eden and the fruitful earth
Which drank in Abel's blood and here in Nod
Refuses her abundance that the birth
Of man first saw. There's talk of sevenfold
And seventy times more revenge, so I—
Like Zillah, Adah, Lamech, Cain—have told
Our children how it is. Why try to lie?
Cain bears the mark but neighbors, whispering
Draw back their skirts from me. Small children call
Like hooting owls while we who bear, unseen,
Our stigma's trace, cannot escape his fall.

The one who killed retains his right to life
While passing, living death, unto his wife.

Genesis 4

WATER WIFE

My ears were ringing with the sound of all
The hammering they did while pitchblende stank,
But when the creatures came without our call
We all trooped in and God pulled up the plank.
For weeks we floated—homeless in our home—
Until one feeding time, some sprouted seeds
Just made my fingers ache to handle loam.
Then God, who spoke to Noah, saw our needs,
Remembered us, and sent his breathing wind.
He hung a rainbow in the misty sky
So that no matter how creation sinned
A flood would never make all nations die.

But with no Garden, eight souls seem so few
To fill the earth and conquer it anew.

Genesis 6—9

HAGAR, THE MAID

My mistress always told me what to do
So when she said, "Here's Abram," how was I,
A purchased servant maid, expected to
Escape? There was no choice but to comply
Without a question raised of rights or love;
And if, as Sarah charged, I grew aloof
I call to witness God who reigns above
That she respected neither me nor truth.
At first she claimed my fruit was on her tree;
Then when her season came, she had no use
For me or Ishmael. In verity
She banished us without a good excuse.

Bad consequences can remain to vex
A selfish calculating use of sex.

Genesis 16 and 21

LOT'S WIFE

I was embarrassed by my husband's greed
When Uncle Abram offered him a choice
Between hard work and riches, without need
Of grinding toil. But then I did rejoice
To have the social life for all our girls
Because I thought ahead of marriages.
At first, I felt some shock to see the curls,
The finery, the gleaming carriages;
But mothers must adjust and Lot was glad
For fertile pasturelands and for new friends
Who call him brother. You can see we had
A good life here, but now you say it ends.
You men are people we don't even know.
Who said you have the right to make us go?

Genesis 13 and 19

LOT'S DAUGHTER

I wonder if my father felt remorse
For offering our virgin bodies to
His fellow Sodomites who came to force
Themselves, in lust, upon the strangers who
Had taken refuge underneath our roof;
Those visitors, in spite of sisters' men
Who mocked, gave all the rest of us the truth
About the home we'd never see again.
Does he remember them, so kind yet grim,
While Mother watered plants and fed the cat?
And now that we are both with child to him
What does my righteous parent think of that?

Although no one will ask the father's name
I look at Baby Moab's face with shame.

Genesis 19

MILCAH

I tried to keep my relatives in sight,
Until each one became a tiny dot
That could be one last glimpse or else just might
Be swirls of sand. Deep down I know that Lot
Is better off in Abram's loving care
But I still like to sit and reminisce
About the happy times we used to share
Before they heard God's call and left. I miss
Them for myself and for the sons I bore
Who never saw their kinfolk face to face.
I think Rebekah needs them even more
To help protect her comeliness and grace.
It seems to me that she was born a queen
And not a desert plant to bloom unseen.

Genesis 11:27-32; 12:5; 22:20-23; and 24:47

SARAH'S THANKSGIVING

Our father, Terah, took us out of Ur
But settled down in Haran. Abram moved
Us on to fill the Promised Land. We were
Still childless and, in haste, I felt behooved
To mate my husband with my maid. That one
Mistake forced us to banish Ishmael
To clear the birthright for our promised son.
And Lord, who kept me safe in harem cell,
I thank you that you knew my feeble strength
And never spoke of sacrifice to me
When I held Isaac to my heart at length.
Because, Jehovah God, in honesty,
Although I traveled patiently through life,
It's hard to be a visionary's wife.

Genesis 16, 20—23

KETURAH

My husband never runs to meet me with
A cry of joy or swings me off my feet
High in the air, but there's contentment if
The second wife equates the ripe with sweet
And never tries to plow a field that she
Should reap. Fresh earth is broken in the spring
By eager partners who expect to see,
In autumn, what rewards their labors bring.
I've nothing new to give to Abraham—
Our marriage is as commonplace as bread.
A tent's a tent and every lamb's a lamb;
I give—not novelty, but peace instead.

The evening star does not compete with noon
Or try, in jealousy, to cloud the moon.

Genesis 25:1-4

REBEKAH

What memories I have of leaving home
To comfort Isaac in his mother's tent,
Of nights we counted stars in heaven's dome
While pondering Jehovah's covenant.
I don't know when we first began to view
The twins with evil partiality;
But seeds, once planted, put out roots and grew
Until a tangle is surrounding me.
How can conspiracy be unconspired
Or half truth, loosely spoken, be made whole?
If pottery could ever be unfired
A liar might escape travail of soul.

I've listened for his step—but now I know
That Jacob will not come before I go.

Genesis 24—28

JUDITH AND BASEMATH

Rebekah is a snoop at best—at worst,
She is a serpent and a sneaking spy
Whose every action is so well rehearsed
That we can never trust what meets the eye.
She hates our idols but she acts like God
Dispensing favor or disdain. The twins
Have not shared equally her love or rod,
But everybody suffers from her sins.
It's bad enough that there are two of us
(Like puppies waiting for our master's word)
Without the burden of Rebekah's fuss
Or fear of things that Esau overheard.

The marriage bed is lumpy for a wife
If parents tangle up her husband's life.

Genesis 26:34, 35; 27:46; and 28:1, 2

ESAU'S MAHALATH

He did not need one more to grind his grain
Or weave protective cloth against the dew,
Because he roams outdoors in sun or rain
And finds his fireside needs are very few.
But he's impulsive—still a willful child
Who fiercely strives to skim the cream from life.
To keep in step with Jacob, sly but mild,
Esau went scrambling for a proper wife.
Already married twice, he added me
To pacify his parents' grief and ire,
Pretending I was aristocracy
Because of Abraham, my father's sire.

I wish my heart had known its future fate,
Before I learned to love my callous mate.

Genesis 28:6-9

LEAH'S LAMENT

You, Rachel, you the ever favored one,
Why can't the watered palm tree be content
To furnish shade? Why pester for a son
When you already know that fate is bent
On serving you with joy and comradeship?
I only heard endearments one night through.
From Jacob's well of love, I got one sip
But every word he said was meant for you.
My helpless longing and my private shame
Of alternating hope and black despair
Are made more public every time I name
My sons—expecting now to be held dear.

I would give anything I have in life
To be my husband Jacob's only wife.

Genesis 29 and 30

DINAH, DAUGHTER OF LEAH

A sister sees her brothers turn to men
Before she joins the women's talk of food,
Of young, of husband's quirks. She wants a friend
Among the girls, and I was in that mood
The day that Shechem watched his father's field
He did not force me, but his touch and words
Were kind until my body begged to yeild.
I did not think of dowry or of herds,
Although my lover bargained as a spouse.
He was in circumcision's agony
When my two brothers looted every house,
Killed all the men, but grabbed the wives and me.
My loneliness could never hurt as much,
If I had lived and died without his touch.

Genesis 34

RACHEL TO LEAH

While facing death, life passes for review:
I see those early days of childlike play
Replaced by rivalry and fears. It's true
I hid our father's gods, and in his way,
Well learned from him, deceived him by a ruse.
But can you, Leah, after years of pain
Imagine how I felt at his excuse
For giving you my wedding veil? In vain
I tried to make him yield the payment due,
But he just fed our jealous fire more wood.
Now Deborah's dead and I must turn to you,
My friend, and enemy, for my son's good.

If poor Ben-Oni lives (I hope he does)
Help him be stronger than his mother was.

Genesis 29, 30, and 35:8, 16-20

TAMAR OF JUDAH'S LINE

Two times, so far, my life was marred by death.
My husband Er, the first in line, God slew
For wickedness, while Onan lost his breath
And right to live when he refused to do
The brother's part according to the law;
But Judah must have issue by God's plan.
Yet as he said, and as I plainly saw,
I'd have to wait till Shelah was a man.
Denied the son, in time, I used the sire.
He said I must be burned for harlotry,
But I said, "Here's my one-day-lover's hire;
My baby's father gave these things to me."

He claimed his staff, his bracelets, and his sign.
"The woman's guilt," he said, "is less than mine."

Genesis 38

SHERAH, BUILDER OF CITIES

What could I do when faced with Father's loss
And knowledge that I could assume the part
Of masculinity to step across
The barriers raised by sex if things of heart
Were tossed aside like withered husks of corn?
I can't bring back my brothers who are dead,
But if my own offspring remain unborn
I might design stone monuments instead.

Now relatives and friends are asking why
I built three cities rather than a house;
They wonder if rooftops against a sky
Can substitute for kisses of a spouse.
Old scars reopen under sympathy
But this remains a chosen path for me.

1 Chronicles 6:66-69; 7:20-24

POTIPHAR'S WIFE

When Potiphar indulgently brought home
The Hebrew slave, he never meant to tease
My flagging appetite or whip to foam
The heavy cream that rose. He meant to please
An unresponsive, well-loved wife who grew
Progressively more cool like fiery flame
Becomes volcanic ash. I wonder who,
In times like these, the gods of romance blame.
Somehow, our Joseph missed slave surgery,
Yet only sees me as his master's wife.
He frustrates me with studied purity,
Castrated by his will—though not by knife.

I tried my best to make him lose his head
And very nearly lost my own instead.

Genesis 39

ASENATH, WIFE OF JOSEPH

Although my childhood held bright hours of play,
The temple shadows often made me quake.
The idol caused my heart no fear by day,
But nightmares used to startle me awake.
Then as my girlish body showed some bloom
I wondered to what man I'd be assigned
And if my marriage would become my doom.
But Joseph holds my body, soul, and mind;
He tells our boys about the ways of sheep
With tender stories of his home, of dreams,
A special coat, and God who needs no sleep.
His love is inexhaustible, it seems.

Before he came, my chance of joy was slim—
My father's god can't make a man like him.

Genesis 41:45

SONG OF THE MIDWIVES

We sing a song of children, ones and tens
Of scores and hundreds, plus uncounted more—
Nobody's lovers, everybody's friends
Because we helped with babies. Sorrow tore
Us both when infants were born dead. But worse
Than stillborns were the healthy ones who died.
We did our best. Sometimes we could reverse
The laws. If not, they had to be defied.
God's future leaders had been saved by us
And solitary parents here and there.
Then quietly, without a public fuss,
He started homes for us, with sons to bear.

Far greater than the wisdom of the wise
Is God, from whom deliverance will rise.

Exodus 1:15-21

JOCHEBED

It seems as though the sun, so long kept out,
Now leaps with joy across the sill—like cats
Who wait for open doors. The children shout
In freedom at their play. While buzz of gnats
And Miriam's lilting song blend in my ears,
My happy fingers trace the royal mark
The princess placed upon our house. Old fears
Have melted since God used my little ark.

The princess was most gracious when I left
My son—and hers—at his new home today.
I kneel beside his empty bed, bereft,
But plan to use my extra time to pray.
At royal schools he'll learn things God can use
But when he's grown, I wonder how he'll choose.

Exodus 2:1-10

PRINCESS OF EGYPT

I love the beneficial Mother Nile
For worship, bathing, and fertility.
Of course I fear her son, the Crocodile,
Whose bloody teeth are schooled in cruelty
Used often now, since Father made his law
About the Hebrew boys. My drawn-out one
Is special. There's no way to save them all
But his wet nurse and I preserved my son.
Without his foster mother he would die
Or without me. He must learn everything
From magic arts, from earth and from the sky
Because he'll someday reign as Egypt's king.

O God of ancient lore and hidden ways,
Help Moses be your servant all his days.

Exodus 1 and 2:1-10

ZIPPORAH, WIFE OF MOSES

My first reaction held both joy and dread
At temper, kindliness, and foreign garb,
But then with some contentment, Moses led
My father's flocks with me. He shared the barb
Of mission which was festering—a thorn
That stuck when planted by his mother's God
Who saved and nourished him when he was born.
In time, I bore his sons; he used my rod.
But there as one vexation in our life—
He had a bloody custom that was done
To infant boys—just eight days old. As wife
And mother, I could spare our second son.

I saved my man; I used the cutting stone—
To rule God's house, he had to rule his own.

Exodus 2:15-25 and 4:24-26

MIRIAM'S THANKSGIVING

I often left my fun to play with him
And quiet every whimper from his bed
Lest baby-hunters by design or whim
Should find out where he lay. He would be dead
According to the Pharaoh's plan—not God's
Who favored little brother from his birth;
So while our men folks bore the bricks and rods,
I helped my mother teach God's man, his worth.
When as his helper, I—and Aaron too—
Because of lesser honors, felt abused
And told our younger brother what to do,
We learned by Moses' love why he was used.

I'm glad, in spite of all the times I fell
That God made me a gift to Israel.

Exodus 1 and 2:1-9; Micah 6:4

ELISHEBA, WIFE OF AARON

One night he said good-by and went to find
His brother, Moses. I was then the least
Of his concerns, but packing kept my mind
From other things. He joined us for the feast
Before the hurried flight with our four sons
And all God's people, leaving Egypt. I
Began to live in fear of God, when ones
Who worshiped Aaron's calf were killed. Then my
Two sons who offered their own fire were dead—
Devoured by God's flames. The change in me
From pity for myself to joy instead
Came when God made my husband's rod a tree.

O God, who strengthens leaders for their task
I'm glad you answer leaders' wives who ask.

Exodus 6:23; 32:19-35; and Numbers 17

SHELOMITH

My husband was not born of Abraham
But was the best Egyptian that we knew,
So we were glad to share with him both lamb
And shelter when the plague of death passed through.
He joined our people and was saved by blood.
Dry-shod, he saw the waters stand apart
Where later, horsemen floundered in the flood.
But we were never truly one in heart,
And now my husband spurns me. All alone
I crumple in my grief and wonder why
Some eat the meat while others gnaw the bone
And why, with my son dead, I cannot cry.

The stones which struck his body also broke
My heart, long-harnessed in unequal yoke.

Exodus 12:37,38 and Leviticus 24:10-16, 23

EXECUTION OF THE SEDUCERS

Like hordes of locust strip the countryside,
We thought the Israelites would kill us all
The day that Balaam and our husbands died
But we were torn away and watched them fall.
From suckling babies to our girls in bloom
The children traveled with us like a herd
Of sheep which goes to pasture or to doom
Depending on the shepherd's final word.
When virgins all were taken first, we knew
That they would meet the fate of concubines
While we would reap a harvest, overdue,
And drink the crushings from our bitter vines.
The curse which Balak tried to buy with gold
Has been reversed upon us, many fold.

Numbers 31:1-24

RAHAB, SALMON'S WIFE

They came at night, as customers would do
But in a moment I could see that this
Was not a business call. They were the two
Most courteous of men. I could not miss
The chance to save my kindred young and old,
And so I made them promise for the Lord
That they would spare my gathered-in household
And I would keep our secret of the cord.
I had a tent and learned to pitch it well
Until—Jehovah's mercies never cease—
I got to be a wife in Israel
And, by my husband's lineage—Aaron's niece.

I'm glad God looks at what a person does
And judges who I am—not who I was.

**Joshua 2 and 6; Exodus 6:23; Numbers 7:12;
and Ruth 4:20-22**

ACSAH, DAUGHTER AND WIFE

Our camp is like a forest of young trees
Where Joshua and Father soar alone
Like two strong cedars standing firm to please
The Lord. For Father, trials served to hone
A sharper, cutting edge of faith to use
In conquest of the Promised Land. What's more,
At eighty-five, he never did excuse
Himself from working hard or waging war.
According to his offer of my hand
For any man who led the battle strife,
Dear Othniel and I received good land
With springs, when I became the hero's wife.

But I remember best that Father's eyes
Saw me as precious—fit to be a prize.

Joshua 14:6-15 and 15:13-19

DAUGHTERS OF ZELOPHEHAD

Because our Father's gone, the years look bleak
With five of us to marry, hopefully,
And no male relatives that care to speak
For us, or save our lives from drudgery.
We've gathered manna with the rest and pitched
Our tent as well as any man, but now
We need some help, or we will all be nitched
In corners where the folks make room somehow.
We feel our worth and know we are as good
As those who keep a clean and happy house,
But where's a modest way by which we could
Attract, for each of us, a worthy spouse?

We praise Jehovah who has made it known
That single girls need land to call their own.

Joshua 17:3-6

DEBORAH

Accumulated wisdom through the years
Unfolding like palm leaves from my own tree
Has helped me make decisions, handle fears,
And triumph in the work God gave. When we
Were frightened off the main highways and hid
Like rabbits in a hole, then God said, "Go
With Barak; he won't go alone." I did,
Although, as wife and mother, I don't know
The general's part or how to wield a sword;
But we, together, with ten thousand men
Saw chariots run, like mice, before the Lord.
Then I went home to Lappidoth again.

When God selects the one he wants to ask
He gives ability to do the task.

Judges 4 and 5

JAEL, WIFE OF A KENITE

I was attracted by the Kenite's lore
As insects seek and circle open flame.
They live among our tribes and furthermore
Had once been Moses' in-laws, just the same
As they are mine. But Heber cut our tie
To pitch his tent outside their camp. My spouse
Made Jabin first a friend and then ally;
Poor flitting bat—he's neither bird nor mouse.
Sometimes, when he would visit Canaan's king
My lonely thoughts would work like rising dough,
But I could never seem to plan a thing
Until that day I struck my deadly blow.

A girl in love may disregard her clan,
Then find it means much more than her own man.

Judges 1:16 and 4:11-24

MOTHER OF SISERA

How dare the moonlight sweep beneath our gate
Before my Sisera comes flashing in
From slaughtering those Hebrew sheep. It's late
And I had thought that he would quickly win
With chariots of iron and horses trained
To scatter men on foot, like quail. We heard
With scorn of Barak. Yet, my son's detained
By someone. Very soon he'll send us word.
The spoil should be divided now. Two slaves
For him, one maiden for another. Cloth
Embroidered on both sides, he always saves
For me—Oh, fear, stop fanning like a moth.

Is there no word of hope or sure relief
For window-watching women, fearing grief?

Judges 5:28-30

JEPHTHAH'S DAUGHTER

My father promised, so there is no chance
For me, unless I'd make him break his vow
To God. I had no way to know my dance
Of joy could spring a trap of doom. But now
I must return—while feeling like a brook
Whose waters will not ever join the sea,
Or like a fuzzy eaglet in a nook
Whose wings will never grow to set it free.
I wonder who will finger those designs
That Father carved into my ivory bed
And if they'll find that no one really minds
My little puppy's mischief when I'm dead.

I hope God has a meadow in the sky
For us who leave the earth too young to die.

Judges 11:30-40

MOTHER OF SAMSON

Our hearts ascended with the angel's flame
Till he evaporated from our sight
And left us with our wonder but no name
For him or for our future child who might
Deliver Israel for the Lord. Our joy
Increased with gratitude that God had shown
His own prophetic will about our boy
And gave him power none of us had known.
Then grapes, forbidden, turned to wine of wrath
Because our son persistently would seek
For honey in a hornet's nest—a path
To prison where he's shorn, and blind, and weak.
When we remember Samson, young and strong,
Our minds keep asking, "Where did we go wrong?"

Judges 13—16

DELILAH'S REGRET

The Hebrew man, with country charm and ways
Of pleasing that I never knew, was still
My enemy. The busy nights and days
Were pieces of a master plan to kill
The happy fly while keeping from his sight
My secret spider web. Of course by law
Poor Samson's downfall was the only right
And patriotic duty that I saw.
I'm wealthy now, renowned, and booked ahead
By politicians, priests, and famous men
Yet I would rather have him free instead.
I would not be so treacherous again.
But time has healed my wound—or so I thought
Until that day I cracked the vase he brought.

Judges 16:4-21

MICAH'S MOTHER

To get that many shekels took my days
And nights while little Micah played nearby
Depending on my job. The varied ways
Of nature passed unseen. The painted sky
And flowered field were wasted in my life.
We did not marvel at the rain or ask
How far a floated leaf would go. As wife
And mother, I did every standard task,
But all the while, I missed the present joy
For silver that the future might require.
I taught materialism to my boy
And now we huddle by a burned-out fire.

When it's too late to change the past, I see
That Micah really needed more of me.

Judges 17—18:26

THE LEVITE'S CONCUBINE

I wish I never would have come along
With him in spite of all the kindliness
He showed in conversation. Warnings—strong
And menacing at night—would seem much less
Important when the sun was high and he
Could be persuaded to postpone again
Our final leaving—which was hard for me,
But nothing like the hardship of these men.
How could he offer me, to serve their lust
While knowing I have been afraid of him?
A woman has to do the things she must,
But times like this can overflow the brim.

I'm crawling back to find his step. I know
That he's no help, but where else could I go?

Judges 19

114

VIRGINS OF JABESH GILEAD

We are like gleanings of a well-cut field
In which the reapers left no standing grain
Because, like Benjamites who would not yield
The rapist-killers, people felt no pain
In Jabesh when they knew perverted men
Went free. All other tribesmen marched as one
And swore to kill whoever would defend
The lust of sodomy which had begun.
Indignant fathers vowed they'd never give
Their girls in marriage to the Benjamites.

When soldiers shook our city like a sieve
Most people lost their lives; we lost our rights.
Now that the sons of Gilead have failed
We envy Jephthah's daughter, long bewailed.

Judges 20:1—21:15

VIRGINS OF SHILOH

We danced at Shiloh in our maiden bloom
(A virgin dance with expectations high)
While gauzy garments, woven on a loom
Of hope, made each of us a butterfly.
We sang along the road to Shechem where
Poor Dinah tasted brief, ill-fated love
And thought of Jephthah's daughter held so dear
But made, by oath, a sacrificial dove.
Then suddenly the air, perfumed by grape
And vineyard fragrance, shattered with our screams,
While every step we ran in fear of rape
Removed us further from our rainbow dreams.
O God, what can the helpless victims say
When men make vows that women have to pay?

Judges 21:16-25

ORPAH

Our sleepy village woke if visitors
Began to climb our winding, rocky way
So now, although most memories are blurs
I still can see the details of the day
Naomi came. Of course, when I met her
I never dreamed that I would be the wife
Of one my people labeled, 'foreigner'.
Nor that his death would devastate my life.
Another son from her is, as she said,
Not really now a possibility;
In spite of love, I will return instead
And hope that there is future rest for me.

The bread of yesterday will not suffice
If here today, I have no loaf to slice.

Ruth 1

RUTH TO NAOMI *AFTER OBED*

I still remember you on that first day
With sweat streaks on your face and wilted from
The dusty road. I wanted you to stay
And use our village as your shelter. Some
Of us were watching how you calmly talked
Among yourselves with gentleness and I
Was most impressed by how your husband walked
Beside you and my heart could feel the tie.
Then as I joined the circle of your love,
Your inner flame warmed me and helped me see
That loyalty and truth form bonds above
My childhood thoughts and last eternally.

I came to share your bitter dregs with you
And found the cup was filled with joy for two.

Ruth 1—4

NAOMI *AFTER OBED*

In happiness and health I felt my life
Was moving like a quiet stream where sheep
Could safely wade. To be a chosen wife,
I found, was like a pond, so clear and deep
That quietness could reign. When God gave sons
He taught us that the ripples catch the light
And streams with hidden music are the ones
That tumble over rocks. Then came the night.
I felt deserted on a beach of sand,
Until in Moab each son found a bride
And briefly shared his home. By death, the hand
Of God once more swept joy and hope aside.
Through Ruth, I see that life is like a shore
And joy can sweep where grief tides ran before.

Ruth 1—4

PENINNAH, HANNAH'S RIVAL

Although my man is good and knows the law
So he does not diminish food or clothes
Or duty of the marriage bond, I saw
Again how he, by worthy portion, shows
In public that she is much more preferred.
But I can nurse my babies in her sight
And by well-chosen toss of head or word
Make sure she shares my shadow day and night.
I think of Zilpah, Bilhah—concubines
Or wives, by name, but not by what we mean.
We know a barrenness—there are two kinds!
The one, we feel, when we give birth or wean.

In spite of pretense, sham, and outer life
There's pain in every loved-by-duty wife.

1 Samuel 1; Genesis 30:1-13; and 33:1-6

HANNAH

To want a child like deserts long for rain
And have a restlessness like ocean's tide
Would be enough, if private. But the pain
Of mean Peninnah's gloating, throbs beside
The knowledge that in cruelty she spoke
So everyone would know. A man can sow
Good seed in willing earth and wait in hope,
But only God has power to make it grow.
That's why I went to him with breaking heart
For fruit and for the clearing of my name.
Praise God, he heard. Now I must do my part
So that my son will never bring us shame.

The way I spend these years that fly so fast
Will make me full or empty when they're past.

1 Samuel 1 and 2

MOTHER OF ICABOD

Of course, I know my husband lies around
With other women in the temple yard,
But that, to me, is not sufficient ground
To hold my vows to God in less regard.
A puppy knows when he's been kicked, but wags
His friendly greeting just the same. I will admit
My old enthusiasm sometimes lags—
Our baby's due without a name for it.

God's ark, my husband, Eli—all are gone:
That is as hard for me to comprehend
As if it were the drowning of a swan.
O, Icabod, the glory's at an end!
My heart has died so many times before,
I'm glad that after this, death is no more.

1 Samuel 4:19-22

AHINOAM, WIFE OF SAUL

It was a scary thing when I was young
To think of marrying a man whose base
Was Gibeah of infamy. I hung
Between my choices trying hard to face
Unknown realities till I was sure
That Saul held happiness for me inside
His gentle hand. At first our love was pure,
Like his for God, before sin made him hide
And turn against the people and the aims
He once held high. He lost his early joys
And Samuel's guidance, turned to witchcraft games,
Then war—which claimed his life and our three boys.

As workmen cut a tree—blow after blow—
Repeated sin has brought God's giant low.

1 Samuel 14:49, 50

ABIGAIL

How can two men both made of common clay,
Both carried for nine months and loved and fed,
And both from Judah's tribe, turn out this way
With David such a prince—divinely led
In contrast to my husband's churlish life?
When David made a reasonable request
And Nabal thundered, "No," I, as his wife,
With prudence, did what I considered best
By letting my man sleep, all stupefied,
Until he woke to hear how narrowly
We all escaped—and was so stunned he died,
Thus clearing things for David and for me.

I tried my best to keep the peace because
We all are hurt by what the husband does.

1 Samuel 25

WITCH OF ENDOR

These hands have mastered chores they never knew
Before, and vegetables are growing in
My patch, because when Saul was asking who
The witches were to kill them for their sin
I was a former witch that very day
With my own goat to milk and hens to feed,
As I began to live a better way
Of freedom from the devil and from need.
But now, with fear, I face the sudden fact
That flashed across my mind when Samuel spoke:
My power with the spirits is intact
And I am locked into a double yoke.

It's too late now, for me. I can't negate
The deal with Lucifer that sealed my fate.

1 Samuel 28:3-25

NURSE FOR MEPHIBOSHETH

To be a nursemaid for the king is hard
Because his children are in danger day
And night. When they are playing in their yard
I'm like a hen with chicks and always pray
That neither dangers from the earth nor sky
Will change their vibrant health or introduce
A threat to life or limb. I hear each cry
With dread lest enemies are on the loose.
And then it happened as I feared it would—
One night—when all the children were in bed.
I snatched Mephibosheth and what I could
Of things he'd need—then dropped him as I fled.

Through years of sorrow, I've bewailed his fate:
Because of my misstep, he can't walk straight.

2 Samuel 4:4 and 9:3-13

BATHSHEBA WHISPERS

The tree Uriah planted in our yard
I see in moonlight from my present house.
Entranced by breezes in his tree, it's hard
For me to sort my thoughts of him—the spouse
Who loved his king and battle comrades more
Sometimes than me. Or so at least it seemed,
Until the death of David's son made sure
Some things of which I'd only vaguely dreamed.
When God sent Nathan, who exposed our wrong,
He made us deal in truth instead of lies.
So now my faith for Solomon is strong;
O God, please use my life to make him wise.

I can't feel guiltless for our trysting night;
My bathing never should have been in sight.

2 Samuel 11:1—12:24

TAMAR

When we were young, we children were a crew
Of happy playmates on the palace ground;
Though born of varied mothers, we all knew
Security in Father and we found
Companionship in our own house. Of all
The relatives, my brother Ammon seemed
Most kind, so when one day I got his call
To visit him at home I never dreamed
Of foolishness and sin. He wanted wine
From summertime of harvest, with no spring
Of wakening or caring for the vine,
And would not wait for blessing from the king.

The man who gets his wish by brutal force
Is prone to then discard without remorse.

2 Samuel 13:1-20

MICHAL

Sometimes I wish I'd let my father's men
Just kill my husband since my saving him
Cost me so much. If we had shared a den
As refugees, I think the chance is slim
That Father could have been thrown off the trail;
So I stayed home and starved my heart each day
While he collected wives—the mighty male—
Until reluctantly, I went away
By force, with Father's choice—a husband who
Then won my heart by gentle touch and word.
When David sent for me, we tried anew,
But words of bitterness changed love to curd.

It takes much more than living in one house
To make a man or woman be a spouse.

**1 Samuel 19:9-17; 2 Samuel 3:12-16; and
2 Samuel 6:17-23**

BELEAGUERED BY WAR

We cannot stand to see armed men outside
Our wall and know that they have come for war,
Expecting to involve those who abide
In peace and harmlessness. And what is more,
Though women are the ones who wait in vain
For sons and husbands from the battlefield,
It's worse when selfishness brings seige and pain
Right to our household doors. We will not yield
Or sacrifice those loved since their first move
Within the womb before we'd swaddled, fed,
And cherished them. It therefore does behoove
A man attacking homes to watch his head.

The battles usually are fought by men
But it's not wise to raid a grizzly's den.

Judges 9:50-55, and 2 Samuel 20

WISE WOMAN OF TEKOA

In family life the people, high and low,
Are equally made vulnerable it seems
Because in every home the members know
The conflict of their love and hate. The dreams
Of perfect unity do not come true
Where sons of Adam each pursue their needs
And individual passion makes them do
The crimes that entered Eden with its weeds.
King David saved my bloody-handed son
Although the guilt was plain, and then he sent
Permission to his long-lamented one
For Absalom's return from banishment.

No parent should behave unnaturally
Because of what the public hopes to see.

2 Samuel 14:1-24

TEN ROYAL CONCUBINES

Conspiracy and flight left us in charge
Of David's palace when he fled unshod
With all the rest, while anyone could barge
In where we huddled—be he prince or clod.
They pulled us out like rabbits from a hole
And Absalom wrought shame beneath a tent
In public view. To purchase his new role
As self-made king, we were the coins he spent.

While years of our confinement stretch ahead
As though we all were guilty of some crime,
Our guards, by order, see that we are fed
Until death will release us all, in time.
But we, as chattel women, spend our days
In ward, while flocks and herds go out to graze.

2 Samuel 15:16; 16:20-23; and 20:3

THE WILLING WENCH

Ahithophel avenged Bathsheba's shame
When Absalom so openly disgraced
His father's concubines and royal name
While barefoot David fled in weeping haste.
Now spies and counterspies lurk out of sight;
Two men who feign allegiance stay at court
And learn how Absalom intends to fight—
But they need help to carry their report.
No wife or daughter from this priestly house
Can safely leave the city undisguised.
But I, a bonded wench, drab as a mouse,
Will use the liberty of one despised.

Nobility, when measured by the deed,
Is not confined to those of noble seed.

2 Samuel 17:1-17

WOMAN IN CONSPIRACY

What could a helpless woman do to save
A king who fled barefooted and uncrowned
Because his son (who never did behave
Except in ways his own desires had found
Were pleasant) had decided to be king?
The haughty Absalom had carved a stone
As his memorial of pride. The thing
He now was coveting was David's throne.

Praise God, who had a part for me to play
When messengers fled to our yard in fear.
My grain, when spread in careful disarray,
Obscured the fact that fugitives were here.

A woman who stays home and bakes her bread
Can sometimes help a man to keep his head.

2 Samuel 17:15-22

SISTERS OF DAVID

Old Samuel shook the elders of our town
When he appeared to make a feast to God,
Insisting that we call our David down
For some strange pouring on of oil. A rod
And staff were wielded in our brother's hand
Which also was as skilled with harp or sling
Before his sword play made a grateful land
Respect and honor him above its king.

As finest wool can be destroyed by moth—
If unprotected—so our peace was marred
When Joab and the rest put on the cloth
Of soldiers and their tender hearts grew hard.

The battles which we women glorified
Have lost their luster since our own sons died.

**1 Chronicles 2:13-17; 1 Samuel 16, 17, 18:1-7;
2 Samuel 2:18-32; 3:22-39; and 20:1-10**

RIZPAH

I could not bear to watch or look away
From seven swinging ropes against the sky
In Gibeah on execution day
When sons of mine—and Merab's—had to die
Because of Saul's mistaken zeal. It's rare
To find a man exacting so much pain
From all who suffered love while he was here
And still seek their escape from him in vain.

With scant protection from the rock—none from
The sky—I chase the jackals and the birds
By night and day while I'm ignored by some
And ridiculed by others with hard words.
But love begins before a child's first breath
And when it's needed, serves him after death.

2 Samuel 21:1-14

ABISHAG FROM SHUNEM

My grandma sang of Saul's great victories
And David's even greater ones, but I
In times of peace have hillside memories
Where grapes and vineyards, sheep and shepherds, lie
Sun-drenched in quietness. When David's scout,
In search of virgins, stopped me as I fled
He would not let me stay or talk about
My shepherd lover or our plans to wed.
I hear each whisper and I see each nod;
They wonder who'll get me when David dies.
I wonder too, but now I'm called by God
To feed this toothless lion who can't rise.

Because of me, he never is alone.
My loving service makes his bed—his throne.

1 Kings 1:1-4, and 2:13-25

THE HARLOT MOTHER

We lived and worked together in one house
And had our babies just three days apart.
But when she claimed my child, I felt a douse
Of icy water overflow my heart,
Because I had no way to prove that I
Was not the one who overlaid my child.
The king heard each of us give her own cry
And grew more quiet as we grew more wild;
Then in a voice of stern command I heard
Him order execution of my son.
The sword was brought, before my frantic word
Of protest made me judged the truthful one.

Sometimes a mother keeps her child from harm
By trusting him to someone else's arm.

1 Kings 3:16-28

SOLOMON'S FAVORITE WIFE

I'm now the queen of Egypt's former slaves,
And Solomon is in the curious spot
Of knowing he's secure if he behaves
According to Jehovah's laws which blot
Out gods like mine, and all the myriad host
His other wives adore. His palace yard
And groves are ecumenical. We boast
That here no deity is ever barred.
I do not have to join the harem strife
Because to anyone it's plainly seen
That Solomon makes me his favored wife,
But every hive should only have one queen.

Although I'm glad I own a splendid house,
My heart would rather have a live-in spouse.

1 Kings 7:7-12 and 2 Chronicles 8:11

THE QUEEN OF SHEBA

As Queen of Sheba, how could I find out
The truth of rumors that I'd heard. It's hard
For anyone to estimate about
The wealth and wisdom of a man unmarred
By war, and still unspoiled by all he owns,
Who made the cedars and the silver be
As plentiful as sycamores and stones
Before he even got his gift from me.
I came to secretly find out the truth
Of all the fairy tale reports, and thought
That he might proudly hold himself aloof
And coldly answer questions people brought.
But great men are the kindest, so they say,
And I found Solomon to be that way.

2 Chronicles 9:1-12 and 1 Kings 10:1-13

WIFE OF JEROBOAM

He could contrive imaginary gods
When politics and kingdoms were at stake,
But with our son so sick, my husband plods
In mental valleys where the buzzards make
Their patient, measured wheelings in the sky.
At Jeroboam's word, I have to go
To find out if our son will live or die—
And who else but the man of God will know?

I shrank back from the prophet's scalding word
And melted like a candle on his floor.
I cannot change the message that I heard;
Our boy will die when I approach my door.
My journey home winds up his life like thread
And just before I reach him, he'll be dead.

1 Kings 12:25-33 and 14:1-20

MAACAH, WIFE OF REHOBOAM

My foolish husband, Rehoboam, lost
Respect and loyalty from angry tribes
When arrogance, like tiny sparks, was tossed
Into the ripened grain. He heard their jibes
But did not take them seriously until
His tax collector's bill was paid in stones.
Our Grandpa David's efforts to instill
God's values failed, but Asa now atones—
Or tries to. He insists that I cannot
Be Mother Queen—nor can my idol stand.
He has declared that sodomy's a blot
Which he's begun to purge from off the land.

In short, I and my systems are undone
By resolutions of my own grandson.

**1 Kings 15:9-13; 2 Chronicles 11:18-23;
and 2 Chronicles 15:16, 17**

WIDOW OF ZAREPHATH

The prophet asked me for a drink, and I
Turned willingly to fetch my water gourd;
But when he wanted bread that was for my
Poor son's last bite before he died, the Lord
Was called to witness that I had no cake,
But only barrel-scrapings of some meal
And one small failing cruse of oil. "Just take
These meager remnants of your food and deal
In kindness—baking first a cake for me,"
He said, "and everything will last until
It rains." His God is merciful, I see,
To resurrect from death instead of kill.

I did not always do the things I should,
But now I'd do life over if I could.

1 Kings 17:8-24

AZUBAH, WIFE OF ASA

Possessively, I wake and watch him sleep
Almost in disbelief. I lift my man
In supplication too, that God will keep
Him safe from every diabolic plan
With which the devil may retaliate
For Asa's turning Judah back to God
And throwing idols down. I fear the hate
From displaced Sodomites who felt his rod
Of righteous indignation. Like a knife
My terror wants to clip his eagle wings
Till I remember I am just his wife;
But he is subject to the king of kings.

I wonder if all men who fill a throne
Have proud and fearful wives who feel alone.

1 Kings 15:9-24 and 2 Chronicles 14, 15, 16

THE WIDOW WHO HAD DEBTS

My husband slighted business in his zeal
For God and it is possible he owed
This bill. It's hard, before my heart could heal
From loss of him, to face this crushing load
Of sorrow for my boys, as though a cart
Wheel weighted heavily is pressing me.
Perhaps the man of God can take my part
And help me keep my sons alive and free.

I praise the Lord who multiplied my oil
And kept it flowing like a golden wave
To free my sons from bonds and slavery's toil,
Plus extra living money we can save.
I thank the Lord that he will bare his arm
To keep a widow's family from harm.

2 Kings 4:1-7

HOSTESS OF SHUNEM

The passing prophet now stops here for bread
Since I, at first, constrained him when I saw
With deep respect his age and balding head,
And thought to make a room upon our wall
Where he could feel that he had found a nest,
In readiness, each time that he came back.
And when he wondered what reward was best
For me, I truthfully could feel no lack.
But that was changed when we received the son
He promised. Evening time demands no light
Until the candle's lit, but once begun
And then snuffed out, its absence brings on night.

Since we saw life and death, we now know more
About the Lord of life, who can restore.

2 Kings 4:8-37 and 8:1-6

NAAMAN'S CAPTIVE MAID

At first my heart was all caught up in fears
When I would wake, not knowing where I was,
And thoughts of home would bring on sudden tears
While I would do the chores a servant does,
Remembering how Mother taught me things
I knew. Then as it healed, my heart could grieve
For Naaman's leprosy which strikes both kings
And slaves but which Jehovah can relieve.

My master lost his leprosy and pride
In Jordan's River. Now his skin is clean
Like his new heart. Although the king, beside
Him in the House of Rimmon, has to lean
On Naaman, we both worship Israel's God
Before an altar made of Israel's sod.

2 Kings 5

NAAMAN'S WIFE

How can you help a husband who is sick
When courage is so strained you almost die
And questions from your friends cut to the quick
While you keep grieving? But you always try
For some communication through a wall
That's built with bricks of pride and mortared tight
With fear. Our little slave says we should call
Upon her prophet's God to make things right.

The sounds of joy were like return from war
With booty richer far than anything
He ever brought from Israel before
On any other mission for his king.

In touch, once more our happy household kneels
Before an altar to the God who heals.

2 Kings 5:1-19

REMORSEFUL MOTHER

No other hate can equal that I feel
Toward my companion in this house of woe.
We had no man to bring a pinch of meal,
For neither of us was one roebuck's doe.
The men by whom we had been loved and fed
Now stayed at home with wives they once denied,
In hopes of getting their small crust of bread,
While our two sons just lay, near death, and cried.
Life, as I felt it ebb, became so sweet
I could not let it go and say good-by
To earth, and with no other food to eat
It seemed most fitting that my son should die.
But now I know that I, who gave him breath,
Survive in shame because I caused his death.

2 Kings 6:24-29

JEZEBEL

My husband, Ahab, was a spineless man
And floated weakly with the tides. In league
With Baal, I taught him when and how to plan
His strategy, refuse to pout, but rig
The circumstances, justify the means,
And further his own cause without a loss
To him, like those dramatic vineyard scenes
Which taught traditional Naboth who is boss.

In spite of all my guards, Elijah came
To frighten Ahab with his prophesy
Of gory judgments in Jehovah's name,
Which turned the king without affecting me.
My final chance for change had disappeared
When bargains with the devil left me seared.

1 Kings 21 and 2 Kings 9:30-37

QUEEN ATHALIAH

Now that my son the former king is dead
I'll just exterminate the royal seed
And put the crown of Judah on my head
Before I hint of any change. I'll need
A few well-seasoned, bloody men to clear
The world of heirs and rid me in one day
Of any competition I might fear.
We'll move so swiftly none will get away.

How after years of reigning as a queen
Could I hear shoutings of "God save the king"?
What does that childlike apparition mean,
And who has engineered this dreadful thing?
It's treason! Treason! Loyalty's at stake.
Have mercy on me, please, for Baal's sake.

2 Kings 11 and 2 Chronicles 22 and 23

HULDAH, THE PROPHETESS

I'm glad my father shared with me the things
That other folks forgot or never knew
About the prophets, priests, successive kings—
Intrigue and evil, idols, and a few
Less public women who fulfilled their roles
Of ordinary life, but also heard
The secrets God reveals to waiting souls
Whose hearts are open to Jehovah's word.
Today Josiah's workmen found the law.
In urgency, bowed down by what they learned,
They trembled to my door for me to call
Upon the Lord of heaven they had spurned.

In time of need God told me what to say
Because I speak to him from day to day.

2 Kings 22:8-20 and 2 Chronicles 34:14-33

JEHOSHEBA, THE AUNT

When Father coldly killed my uncles in
His fear of rivalry, Elijah sent
A letter prophesying that his sin
Would cost his family, but he was bent
On following the ways of Ahab's house.
My one surviving brother was then set
Into idolatry with Father's spouse.
Now Ahaziah's gone. I cannot let
The evil Athaliah blow the flame
From every candle left; I'll salvage one
Of David's line and teach Jehovah's name,
While rearing him in secret with our son.

Because no one can tell how she'll behave,
Heartbrokenly I choose one child to save.

2 Chronicles 21, 22, and 23

FOREIGN WIFE

The thing that makes our separation hurt,
Like hollow teeth, is my remembering
That even when I first began to flirt
I knew these men were subjects of a king
Who was against unequal yokes between
His men and folks like me—a Canaanite
Who violates his laws of what's unclean;
And now our fruitful marriage suffers blight.
The leaders' men have worked the tangles loose,
Deciding when we'd leave and where we'll live,
While helping children see that there's no use
Of saving marriages God can't forgive.

There cannot be solutions without pain
When marriage laws are treated with disdain.

Ezra 9 and 10

BUILDERS OF JERUSALEM

Our heavy days are lightened by the zest
That conflict lends while we rebuild the wall;
And heathen neighbors do their crafty best
To hinder us with threats of force, and call
Insulting slurs of what a fox could do
By running up our masonry. We work
Without a break, and Nehemiah, who
Is ruler, watches enemies that lurk.
Each man has his assignment, with his sons,
And builds while keeping weapons by his hand.
But we, who have no brothers, are the ones
Who work with Father at the Lord's command.

The other workers might not take as long
But when we're done our wall is just as strong.

Nehemiah 3:12

NOADIAH, FALSE PROPHETESS

I'm like a raging storm which rent the night
Then whimpered off into a quiet lull
Before the rosiness of dawning light
Outlined a cedar tree that would not fall.
Recurring nightmares have replaced my dream
Of saving all this land for us. I had
No chance! Sanballat's and Tobiah's scheme
Has caught me in the middle—looking bad.
Old Nehemiah scorned our sabotage;
He built a wall from rubble heaps and set
Up gates. Now that it's finished they can lodge
Beyond the reach of weapons or of threat.

My baffled mind is at a total loss
To fathom how he knew my words were false.

Nehemiah 2:19, 20; 4:1-3, 19-23; and 6:1-14

QUEEN VASHTI

I was his queen and I enjoyed the things
Ahasuerus whispered in my ear.
But acclamation is the way of kings
Who flaunt their treasures and who like to hear
That no one's wealth surpasses what they hold.
Yet my self-consciousness would chill me when
I feared the servants were too close, like cold
Spring wind makes fruit tree buds retreat again.
The day that we were each surrounded by
Our friends was not a time when even crowns
Could tempt a little rabbit—scared and shy—
To venture forth in front of baying hounds.

A woman does herself and others harm
By public exhibition of her charm.

Esther 1

ZERESH, WIFE OF HAMAN

I was as eager as a hound that trails
Small game to sniff out Haman's news of court
And his successes. Asking for details
Of queenly dress and menus, I'd resort
To any measure that gave me a part
In his exclusive closeness to the king,
Although I knew my husband's bitter heart
Was festering into a deadly thing.

With Haman gone, and ten sons murdered in
One day, I cower in an empty house
That's haunted by his gallows and the sin
Of my suggesting them to please my spouse.

A noble wife should take a moral stand
Before her husband's goals get out of hand.

Esther 5:9-14; 6:12-13; and 9:6-13

ESTHER SPEAKS

They say I'm graceful as the willow trees,
But I feel much more like a sturdy oak
That men can burn or split or shape to please
When they have need. Since parents died, I spoke
To cousin Mordecai when I felt
My helplessness. I'm glad it's over now.
Jehovah made Ahasuerus melt
When I was sent to make my virgin bow
To circumstances and to him. Again
When Haman showed his hand, the king took mine
And made a proclamation to all men
Confirming rights of Jews, and fixed his sign.

By now, God's purposes are clearly seen
In having me become a pagan's queen.

Esther

JOB'S WIFE

I was Job's queen of generosity:
The more we gave, the more we seemed to get
Until our wealth surpassed reality
Yet still increased. I never will forget
The picture that the children made as they
Enjoyed their life together, taking turns
For each to entertain the others. Day
By day, Job was the one who felt concerns.

Our life exploded, while I blinked my eye.
I was the only thing God left to Job
And I, repulsed, told him to curse and die;
I played the fool and spurned the mourner's robe.
My soul stands shivering—stripped and alone—
To find that things meant more than I had known.

Job 1:1—2:10

IMMANUEL'S MOTHER

I felt that God confirmed my early choice
To be a virgin prophetess. Yet now
And then, as I would watch new brides rejoice,
I had to pray for strength to keep my vow
So that the Lord could always find my life
Available, without the daily chores
Or worries that are juggled by a wife
Who has no time to enter other doors.
O, how things changed the day Isaiah came
And called me highly favored as the one
God chose to be a sign. He shared a name
Which witnesses agreed was for our son.

So now when neighbors rail and gossips fuss
I whisper to my child, "God is with us."

Isaiah 7:1-16; 8:1-8, and 18

JOB'S DAUGHTERS

We hear folks praise our loveliness and grace,
But Mother says that beauty of the heart
Is more important than a lovely face;
And we have each been taught to do our part
Of churning, weaving, and the cleaning work—
Although we could have servants by the score.
We hide our roughened hands while questions lurk
About some mystery of spoken lore.
Sometimes our parents seem, without a word,
To send each other messages; and we,
From relatives and friends have vaguely heard
That life, for them, was once a leafless tree.
Now, Father passes cups—filled to the brim—
And Mother's faded eyes light up for him.

Job 42:10-17

THE GRATEFUL WOMAN

My house and business, lands and charities,
Keep me so occupied I'm like an ant
Who scurries single-minded. I please
My family in ways that others can't
Because I have the strength I need—and more!
My well-pruned vineyard and my garden yield
The servants' food plus all that we can store,
But I have never had a stony field
Or plow so dull it would not turn the earth.
I sharpen skills and needles (not my tongue)
When neighbors dress in rags and suffer dearth,
Because I care when people plod unsung.
My husband's praise makes home a special place;
I feel he values me—not just my face.

Proverbs 31:10-31

THE CONSTANT LOVER

I've lost all track of time. How long have I
Been living in a room of draperies?
How long before I skip beneath a sky
Of fleecy sheeplike clouds, while grapes and trees
Perfume the air, and my betrothed claims me?
The king, my charge while he drew breath, is dead,
So after days of mourning I'll be free
For lilies, apples, and my nuptial bed.

The guards for Solomon made me return
As though I were inherited along
With David's throne. But inwardly, I yearn
To find my shepherd and renew our song.

Because the king could not destroy my love
I'm flying home—once more, a country dove.

Song of Solomon

JEWISH WOMEN IN EGYPT

That prophet Jeremiah pesters like
Elusive lice that bite and then evade
The scratching fingers. Now he tries to strike
Our hearts with fear and all the fault is laid
At our bare feet. (It's true our children join
In bringing sticks for worship of the queen.)
But there's another side to every coin:
We aren't alone if all the truth were seen.
It's true we kneaded cakes and baked the dough
For Queen of Heaven's worship. But again
We file a protest that the truth would show
Our homage was approved by our own men.

Since Eve first heeded Satan, it's the same;
When things go wrong, the women get the blame.

Jeremiah 44:7-30

DESIRE OF EZEKIEL'S EYES

My husband's interesting. I like to live
Where I can hear about his visions—wild
And full of all the drama he can give.
With pictures of those fiery wheels, a child
Could stay awake at night remembering.
He speaks of scrolls, of cutting hair and vines,
To groups that gather and he knows the king
Of Babylon will follow God's designs.
One time he spent four-hundred-thirty days
Away from home, just lying on one side
In prophecy of future doom. He pays
A heavy price, and though I never chide,
I wonder why he looked so sad and why
He kissed me two times when he said good-bye.

Ezekiel 24:15-18

127

WIFE OF NEBUCHADNEZZAR

The captives looked so pitiful and worn,
Like draggled kittens with no mother's tongue
To groom them, and with childhood ties all torn.
We even changed their names. Those who had sung
The songs of Zion wept, while willow trees
Held idle harps, and sorrow edged our streams
Without a sign of mirth. But one of these
Displaced young men interpreted dark dreams.
Old memories came flooding back tonight
When horror gripped Belshazzar in its hand,
Reminding me that Daniel's God sheds light
On hidden meanings men can't understand.

The son who would not heed his father's fall
Sees his own judgment written on the wall.

Daniel 5 and Psalm 137

GOMER, WIFE OF HOSEA

Hosea loves me faithfully and tends
The babies, sometimes, when he's able to,
So people wonder why I need my friends
When I already have a husband who
Keeps candles lighted while I'm gone; but still
There is a restlessness that prickles me
And hollows little cavities to fill
While scary dreams obscure reality.
He pleads with me for our three children's sake,
But doesn't hear me say that I'm a child.
To be so changeable is hard to take
And thoughts of bars and cages leave me wild.

I'm back, again—paid for in cash and grain.
The clouds are here. How long until the rain?

Hosea 1, 2, and 3

THE CLOUD OF WITNESSES

Our sorrow weeps in all the willow trees
And is distilled in every drizzling rain
While laughter's echoes float upon the breeze
That cools a summer day and eases pain.
When people press a conch against an ear
To catch the pounding rhythm of the sea,
It is our throbbing heart that they can hear,
And to some mysteries, we hold the key.
Our feelings which are soft as kitten fur
Are also sharp as any piercing thorn;
So thoughts of honey mingle with the myrrh
Each time we sense a child is newly born.

But questionings of life are in the past
Now that we know as we are known—at last.

The Author

Barbara Keener Shenk loves people: family, friends, and strangers. She also enjoys studying and teaching. Her bachelor's degree in education and her master's degree in psychology from Millersville State College were separated by almost thirty years. In those years she married her high school sweetheart and took a twenty-year maternity leave.

Now that the eight children are all adults, Harold and Barbara sometimes do team teaching on family and health concerns. They are commissioned as church planters in Lancaster, Pennsylvania, near their home. Her first book, *Rimes for Our Times,* was written for the family as a theology for children.

Professional activities include not only counseling, teaching, and consulting but also guiding tours, writing, and speaking. She serves as resource person on Anabaptist family life for Suffolk University. As she interacts with a variety of people, Barbara believes that her birth and childhood in the isolated Little Britain community of southern Pennsylvania, with its diverse population, was preparing her for her multifaceted life.

The Illustrator

Sibyl Graber Gerig, a free-lance medical, biological, and general illustrator, lives with her husband, Winston, in Cuyahoga Falls, Ohio, where he is completing a surgical residency in nearby Akron.

Born in 1958 in the Pribilof Islands of Alaska, Sibyl grew up in Puerto Rico, where her parents continue to reside. She attended Eastern Mennonite High School, Harrisonburg, Virginia, for two years, received a B.A. in art from Goshen College, Goshen, Indiana, in 1980, and a Master of Fine Arts degree from the University of Michigan, Ann Arbor, in 1983.

Sibyl has illustrated an anatomy and physiology textbook, plus various lab manuals, and her art appears in medical journals. *The God of Sarah, Rebekah, and Rachel* is her first book of general illustrations. Using carbon dust along with carbon pencils, she has achieved a serene, almost mysterious quality. The smooth modulation of forms, a strong emphasis on light and shade, and careful foreground detailing provide a sense of depth and space.

Across the miles, her artist mother (Esther Rose Graber) was an invaluable source of help and encouragement. Sibyl's twin sister, Ann, director of design at Herald Press, was responsible for the overall appearance of the book.